The Executive Diet

Executive Essentials

---

by Thirteen of Today's Thought Leaders

The Executive Diet

Copyright © 2013 of each article and chapter belongs to each of the respected authors.

Compiled and Arranged by Deepak Lodhia and Associates.

Dedication

"This book is dedicated to every hardworking executive that is ready to grow and thrive through changes, challenges, creativity and is willing to contribute to something bigger. These are the essentials of life that make us come alive"- Deepak Lodhia

Table of Contents

Foreword

On the 12th of February 2013, thirteen of today's thought leaders gathered in one room to share ideas.

The Executive Diet was born, Just like any diet requires consistent exercise of new disciplines to get amazing results.

Learn these new disciplines and put them into action intentionally and constantly over the next 90 days and reap the rewards. Why 90 days?

Because it takes 90 days to create new habits.

Introduction

"We are all unlimited beings, limited by the concepts of limitations you hold in mind"- Lester Levenson

Take this opportunity to uncover your limitations allowing you to create unlimited people and results.

Chapter One

Finding Diamonds in Difficult Times
By Deepak Lodhia

"For me the greatest beauty always lies in the greatest clarity."~.Gotthold Ephraim Lessing

I am sure you would agree with me that we live in difficult or interesting times depending on your point of view. Finding diamonds is a lot easier than you think. You see, every diamond is a force of nature created and defined by everyday pressures, just like you. Flawless diamonds are very rare, but real diamonds are true jewels of nature containing flaws making them totally unique, making them priceless.

If you were to explore these diamonds, you would have to consider the four C's, which create the diamond-coaching model:

Clarity
In this time of overwhelming information, our minds have Become cluttered with information and misinformation.

Clarity brings about clearer thinking, which leads to better decisions and better outcomes.

Clarity removes barriers and obstacles that usually stop us taking action towards our dreams and goals. I once asked a group of executives in a meeting , " What is it that stops you achieving your dreams?"

The answers I got back were:

"Fear!'

"Not enough time!"

"Money!"

"Family!"

"Laziness!"

"Perfectionism!"

"Resistance!"

"Overwhelm!"

To which I replied, "Great answers, but not true!"

We took a little time and used the clarity process and it turns out that **NONE** of these answers were true!

The truth uncovered was that they had all become Comfortable and settled for a good life rather than the outstanding life they actually deserved. Strangely enough, the same group became empowered enough to regain their sparkle by gaining clarity over their current situation.

Clarity affects your ability to tackle challenges, embrace changes, to create and innovate as well as contributing to the "Stakeholders" in our dreams. Remember, your dreams are not for sale!

Colour

"The soul is dyed the colour of its thoughts. Think only those things that are in line with your principles and bear the light of day. The content of your character is your choice. Day by day, what you choose, what you think and what you do is who you become. Your integrity is your destiny... it is the light that guides your way." Heraclitus

The colour of your thoughts and beliefs will determine the reality you create. Your beliefs affect your thoughts, which affect your emotional experiences of the world and thus your results, which will either re-enforce your beliefs or reshape them. They will either lead you to a place of "I Can't" or "I Can". Imagine having the ability to take a moment to discover how you could move from a place of I can't to a place of I can about any particular situation in your life. How would you feel?

If we can uncover our beliefs about a particular situation it will allow us to discover our true capabilities or highlight where we have been hiding out as excuses from shining brightly. What would it be like to stop hiding out, and replacing it with living a fully expressed life?

CUT

Life brings us so many unnecessary complications or pressures. Each one of these affects our ability to perform effectively thus reducing our productivity. If we look at the Pareto Principle, also known as the 80:20 rule, it states that a few vital things bring about the majority of the results and the mass of trivial tasks bring about very little in terms of results.

In other words, 20% of what you do brings 80% of your results and 80% of what you do brings only 20% of your total results, yet as most people who are high achievers, we maintain our 20% and focus on the 80% that only brings about a 20% yield. What if we were to **CUT** the 80% and focus on the 20%, our yield would be bigger and we would have so much more time to be productive.

During an executive training, we did an exercise in which we looked at the time we spent answering trivial problems, emails, phone calls and non-productive tasks. I asked the group to plan the day in which this 80% was almost eliminated to allow for time to play, be creative and communicate with their teams. Not only did the teams complain of having too much time on their hands but that productivity went up as well as the general motivation and moral of the team.

I mean imagine that, less work, more time, better motivation and a better result. The Cut of the diamond creates the sparkle in your life, it brings the fire and brilliance in each member of your team.

Carat

The carat of a diamond is the proportional balanced size of the diamond. In order for the carat to bring out the beauty of a diamond it must be proportional and well balanced. Just like in life, however big you want to play in life, make sure it is well proportioned and balanced for your health, wealth and well being.

Balance is absolute key, it creates opportunity for growth and sustainability, which must be planned in a manner to inspire and infect your team. Start with the "Why" you are going to do something before you consider

"What" you are going to do and "How" you are going to do it!

The "Why" drives your "What" which derives your "How".

Most people focus on the "What" and "How" but never on the most important driving factor which is the "Why". The why is what drives our behaviours, which will change our what and how. It will also bring about change in the way we present our ideas and work to the world.

Underlining every why, is an emotional intention which you are trying to fulfil such as being happy, fulfilled, safe and loved. In most instances it is totally unrecognised but decided upon as an end point such as I will be (insert emotion) Happy when I achieve (X).

Moment by moment, you create exactly how you feel, what happens to you, and what you attract into your life. Unfortunately, you're probably doing all this on autopilot. Emotional Mastery is your opportunity to do this consciously and have the life you dream of by managing your emotions.

We all have three eyes, two for looking out of and one for looking within. Why would we want to look within when everything is happening 'out there'?

Because the treasure we seek is inside, not outside. What is treasure? Beauty, truth, peace, happiness?

You already have what you seek. You already are stunningly beautiful. You are already peaceful and loving. How come you don't know this? Simple, you never look inwards, beyond superficial memories or recent experiences, so you never see your own riches. Take a moment to stop, look inside and see. Don't rush. Don't search. Just look. And be aware. Faith is the surest guide in the darkest days.

Only when we find the quietness in our own minds can we begin to hear our inner teacher, so that we may receive some in-tuition. Only when we are ready to recognise and value the wisdom that we carry at the core of our being will we turn our attention inwards and 'listen in'. But it's been a long time since we truly listened, so a little practice and patience will be needed. Sit down, be quiet and listen in at some point today and you might be surprised at what you hear. Then do it again tomorrow. All you need to do is remember that you are the listener and not the noise.

Ego is not just having a 'big head'. Ego is present every time you feel any kind of fear, or hear yourself saying "That's mine!" The truth tells us that nothing is 'mine' or 'yours', we are all trustees, and fear is only

13

present where there is the voice of attachment. So where there is ego, there is attachment, and where there is attachment there is fear, and where there is fear there cannot be love and where there is no love there is misery. This is why there is so much unhappiness in the world. Detach from everything, and you will banish ego and fear will be no more. Only then can true love return, and our oldest friend happiness will feel it is then safe to reappear back into your life.

When the energy of our consciousness is out of our control - the mind is agitated. We are being emotional. The solution is to detach from the inner storms, stand back and observe the hurricane pass. Detached observation withdraws the energy of which your emotions require to sustain themselves. When you watch your own anger, it dies. If you don't detach from it, and observe it ...it will be your master. Today is the day to practice positive, detached observation, and each emotion-filled moment is the opportunity.

This is 'real' work, the work of one who is a master of his or her own consciousness.

Are you a master or a slave?

Are you ready for Emotional Mastery?

Bring together the four elements, Clarity, Colour, Cut and Carat you suddenly become more productive, more attractive and Purposeful.

"Purpose creates an opportunity for value creation. Passion follows purpose. Passion creates energy, money is attracted to energy."

This will allow you to shine like the diamond you are regardless of how difficult the times are.

My question to you is very simple, how will you use this?

Deepak Lodhia is an optimist. He believes in a bright future and our ability to build it together. Deepak specialises in executive dynamics and human behaviours. Deepak teaches leaders and organizations how to inspire people to make the absolute best of their potential, to become fulfilled, productive and profitable.

By Inspiring and engaging with audiences and clients, Deepak has enabled them to tap into that source of potential and use it in a practical rather than theoretical way to make positive changes to their lives.

As a leading international speaker in Emotional Intelligent Decision Making and Author of several books

Deepak has had the fortunate opportunity to train and coach hundreds of people all over the world, to create and live fuller, productive and profitable lives.

Deepak has held a life-long curiosity for why people and organizations do the things they do. Fascinated by the leaders and companies that make the greatest impact in the world, those with the capacity to inspire, he has discovered some remarkable patterns of how they think, act and communicate. He has devoted his life to sharing his thinking in order to help other leaders and organizations inspire action.

Deepak has earned notoriety for his Diamond model, which has caused a stir amongst conventional thinkers. As a qualified pharmacist and member of the Royal Pharmaceutical Society and The General Pharmaceutical Council, Deepak has applied his logical approach to many unconventional situations.

For further details on how to book Deepak contact

Deepak@DeepakLodhia.com

www.DeepakLodhia.com

Chapter Two
7 Habits of Highly Annoying People
By David Thompson

"I love mankind. It's people I can't stand." - Charles Schulz,
Go Fly a Kite, Charlie Brown

After more than 20 years of working across borders and cultures - I've come to discover that the criteria for success are strikingly similar no matter where you are.

The behaviours that deliver sustainably positive results may differ from culture to culture in matters of style or degree - but the essential patterns remain the same. Decisiveness, focus, proactivity, respect for self and others, willingness to listen and the ability to create a compelling vision of the future tend to do the trick — regardless of the particular company or country in which you find yourself.

But I've also found that the patterns that can hold people back - or, to be more direct about it, the behaviours make some people a complete pain the ass - also appear with striking similarity all over the world.

Do note that I haven't called this chapter THE 7 Habits of Highly Annoying People . . . because that might suggest that there are *only* seven patterns of behaviours that make someone highly annoying. On the contrary, as we all know from personal experience, the universe continuously reveals infinite possibilities for people to get on each other's nerves.

The seven patterns I've selected are the ones I see with alarming frequency in the workplace – especially the workplace of the modern multinational corporation. They're such common – and, in most cases, such unconscious – behaviours that the vast majority of the people who use them don't even realize that they're winding the rest of us up.

Labelling

You remember how, in school, nearly everyone was slotted into a different category? Footballers, swots, drama queens, computer geeks, stoners, skivs, posh gits, pram-faces, etc. You'd get a label, become associated with a certain group of people (or not, if you were a loner or weirdo) – and the label would stick. For years.

Most of us would like to think we've grown out of such limiting behaviours, but just listen to the kind the comments people make about each other in the modern workplace:

"Careful about him – he's difficult."
"Now that one's a top performer!"
"She's not really leadership material; too emotional."
"Oh don't get me started on those HR people."
"What do you expect? He's French[1]."

Whether they're positive terms like 'top performer,' or 'hard worker,' or (as is more often the case) less flattering appellations, labelling other people is a highly annoying habit with hugely frustrating results.

---

[1] There are plenty of people who will tell you that knowledge of cultural differences is critical – and there's value in that information. But too often, that leads to people taking lazy shortcuts grouping entire populations under a single descriptor. And that's pretty racist when you think about it. Next time you're about to make a sweeping generalisation about "the Italians," or "the Chinese," quickly substitute the nationality you're describing with terms like "the blacks" or "the Jews." Your previously innocuous comment now sounds pretty stupid and offensive, doesn't it? But the mental process of saying "the French," or "the Germans" is the same. The point is to think through your large-scale assumptions more carefully – deal with the *person*.

Once you've applied a label to someone – or accepted another person's description of someone else – you'll wind up finding evidence to support your use of the term.

If you've decided someone's arrogant, then whatever that person does will be read as proof of your good judgement. Did they speak for several minutes in a meeting? Then obviously they're dominating the discussion. How perfectly arrogant. Or did they stay quiet? Clearly, they're just looking down on the rest of us.

The top performer, on the other hand, speaks so much because she's so clever – or remains quiet because she's attentive to what others have to say.

And so on.

This phenomenon is known in psychology as *confirmation bias*, and it explains why it can take us years to let go of prejudices we've formed – even in the face of overwhelming evidence that says we're wrong.

When we use and hold fast to our labels for others we lose focus on what those people are actually *doing* and stay fixed upon our *interpretations* and *evaluations* of what we see.

How to Quit:

First, start paying attention to the labels you're using for the people around you. You don't necessarily need to stop it immediately – just notice the terms you're using and let yourself become aware of their effect. Awareness is the first step.

Next, notice what happens when you lift the label and allow yourself to observe other people in action without judgement. What do you see people do when you don't describe them with either positive or negative terms.

Criticism:

"Now wait a minute!" cries the Critic. "Being critical isn't an annoying habit – it's telling the truth. Sometimes the truth hurts – but you've got to be realistic. Someone's got to tell it like it is. No one can improve if they don't know how they're really doing."

The Critic has a point. It's crucial for shoddy thinking to be challenged and poor performance to be improved. Praise for bad ideas and mediocre work will eventually lead an organisation to become complacent, flabby and weak. But why are the positive intentions behind criticism so rarely apparent?

The Critic's true bad habit is in pointing out what's wrong with something *without offering possibilities for making it better.* The Critic becomes the highly annoying person by turning their (usually public) criticism into a way of showing everyone in the room how much smarter / more experienced / tougher / more cynical they are.

Over time, people don't share ideas, drafts or possibilities for change because they fear the Critic's condemnation. As a result, teams and organisations can become as stagnant, complacent, flabby and weak as if they'd been over-praising each other just for showing up every day.

How to Quit:

Recognise that it's easy to poke holes in other people's work or ideas. The real challenge is to identify how they could become better. Next time you're about to criticise – think about how the other could improve the work in question. Ask questions – politely, not sarcastically – to encourage the other person to expand their thinking. Ask them "how could we make this happen?" "What's the first step to making this work?" Ask, "what are the potential consequences?" If they don't know – you could say, "I'm concerned about XYZ – what do you think?"

Gossip

Everybody loves a bit of juice. There's nothing like a bit of court news – who's in, who's out – to get the tongues a-wagging, unless it's information about *personal* peccadilloes or indiscretions. No matter how busy they might be, certain people always find the time to engage in idle talk about and petty judgements of their colleagues.

The truly artful gossip manages to mask their dishing of the dirt with expressions of concern for the person they're talking about. "I hope Arnaud is OK: I heard he did a really poor job on the presentation. He must be feeling awful." Or, "It's so sad to see Emily like this. Her relationship with her boyfriend has been falling apart since what happened with Tom at the Christmas party . . ."

Anyone who's been the subject of rumours and whispers knows how unpleasant it is to be talked about – especially by people who don't know what they're talking about.

Several years ago, I worked with a married person who had an affair with a colleague. Somehow, word got out around the office – and the man's reputation began to crumble. "How could he do that to his wife? He's got kids!" The woman involved got even shorter shrift. "Homewrecker. Sleeping her way to promotion, obviously . . ." and worse.

But the gossiping hordes only knew part of the story. The man and his wife had agreed to separate, amicably, nearly a year before the 'affair' took place. They were still sharing a house while they sorted their financial affairs and made arrangements for the children. The wife had also started another relationship. Though the situation was awkward and rather unconventional, there was no deception involved – just people getting on with their lives. In other words, the tut-tutters were judging without insight or context.

The point is two-fold. First, don't gossip. Don't say things *about* someone else that you wouldn't be comfortable saying *to* them. Second, when you hear rumours and innuendo – withhold your judgement. You don't know the whole story – and you shouldn't, because it's none of your damn business.

Whining

OK, I know. There *are* serious grievances that need to be addressed at work. Bullying bosses or colleagues, health and safety violations, etc. But in my experience, the instances of genuine issues that required action from HR or legal are an infinitesimal fraction of the vast number of things that people moan about every single day.

Seriously, stop it. No one wants to hear you complain about petty turf disputes or a boss that doesn't truly value you. We've all got stuff to deal with at work. We all feel underappreciated. We're all underpaid. Blah blah blah.

Get some perspective. If you're reading a business book like this, it means you're probably employed (or will likely soon be again) in a professional role that doesn't involve your getting dirty or sweaty or dealing with sluice very often. That makes you absurdly lucky. Having shelter, electricity and a continuous supply of food and running water makes you one of the richest people on the planet.

If you're truly unhappy in your role, do something about it. But please don't moan. We've got work to do.

Giving Advice

You might wonder why giving advice would be

annoying. You're just trying to help, right? But when you drop in with your helpful suggestions for how someone ought to do something – you're more than likely going to get on their nerves right quick. If they're a peer or a superior, and they didn't ask for your input about the font they're using, etc – don't give it.

Now, you caring creature, you're probably wondering about giving advice in more emotionally charged situations – when someone has come to you with a problem. It's OK then, right? Wrong.

When people come to you with a problem that they want to discuss, the vast majority of the time they simply want to be heard. They want to know you're listening – they want someone to acknowledge what they're experiencing. When you jump in with your solution, you're making the interaction about your good ideas rather than about their situation. And that's highly annoying.

When you offer advice off the cuff – and let's face it, that's how most advice is given – you're telling the person that the solution is obvious. You'll wind up making them feel kind of stupid for having not thought of it themselves. Plus, by advancing your solution to their problem, you're taking ownership of and responsibility for it away from them. If your advice works, then they're left beholden to you rather than empowered of their own accord. If it doesn't, then they'll blame you for whatever happens next. So hold back.

How to Quit:

Just listen first. Acknowledge what you're hearing. Give the person time and space to vent. Then ask questions. Ask them what they'd like to have happen. Ask them what they've tried. Ask them what else they could try if they could do whatever they wanted. And see what they come up with. They'll likely surprise you – and themselves – with a better idea than what you might have suggested. And good on them.

Wanting to Win

There comes a time in every heated discussion at work when the original topic or reason for disagreeing gets lost. All parties to the argument seem to transcend the original conflict to reach entirely new heights of disagreement. By this point, nobody's focused on finding the best solution or way forward anymore – now it's become about wanting to win.

We've all been there – that moment when we've

decided that we're not going to concede to that *other* because *they're wrong*. We're not going to cede ground. And at this point the value of the argument has been lost. Good conflict, where people argue passionately for an approach or an idea that they believe will be the best way forward, is healthy and necessary for organisations to thrive.

But when it gets personal – and it becomes a game of status and position – it's time to let it go.

How to Quit:

Again, it's about mindful awareness. As soon as you become aware of your desire to get one over on the other – or to have your way because it's your way – take a breath. Ask yourself whether the real issue is about your ego or about doing what's right for the group. The most effective people know how to assert their point of view (and how to listen well to others) for the good of the whole rather than to feed their need to dominate.

Waiting to Talk

Another one of which all of us have been guilty at one point or another: rather than actually focus on what the other person is saying – in a meeting or in a conversation – we simply wait for our turn to talk. Then, having not listened, we simply recite the script in our heads rather than respond to what the other person has put forward. The conversation either goes off track or becomes stilted or descends into argument – all because we didn't listen. We simply waited for a pause in the action so that we could have our turn to talk.

How to Quit:

Pay attention to the self-talk that's going on in your head while another person is speaking. Then turn down the volume of your internal dialogue and allow yourself to become intensely interested in the other person. Focus on matching their body language – and then, when it is appropriate for you to speak, try to match their words and tone. You'll find that by truly tuning into the other person, your script goes out the window and you wind up saying something of far greater value than the lines you had planned.

So there they are – 7 habits that so often derail meetings, conversations and relationships. I'd love to say I only know them from seeing them in others – but of course

I'm as guilty of them as anyone. The point is that by recognising them, we can choose to change our habits – improving collaboration, interaction and driving far fewer of our colleagues to distraction.

David helps leaders at all levels communicate more clearly, perform more effectively and inspire the people around them. With more than 20 years of experience in corporate communications and business management, David helps clients harness their resources for outstanding performance.

David began his career in communications with Ketchum in Washington D.C., and joined the company's Munich office in 1995. In London, David was a Director of the agency's Corporate Practice Group. He later led a sponsorship consultancy, helping clients engage with arts and educational institutions.

David holds a BA in English Literature from Davidson and

an MA in Shakespearean Theatre from Essex University. In addition to his work as a consultant, coach, trainer and facilitator, David is an experienced actor and director of Shakespeare's plays.

David founded Total Awareness Coaching in 2004 to help clients embrace the opportunities and responsibilities of leadership - at every stage of their careers.

Contact Details:
David Thompson
david@totalawarenesscoaching.com
www.totalawarenesscoaching.com

Chapter Three
Inspiration is Great, Commitment brings Greatness.
By Kevin Mclernon

"life is constantly testing us for our level of commitment, and life's greatest rewards are reserved for those who demonstrate a never-ending commitment to act until they achieve. " Anthony Robbins

Have you ever picked up a book, or attended an event or seminar and been inspired? You might have read an amazing story of overcoming adversity or watched and listened as a speaker shared their story of mountains climbed and oceans swam. You then feel full of enthusiasm, asking yourself 'if that person is capable of such greatness, success, and unwavering belief what could I be capable of doing? Something inside of you feels inspired to climb your own mountain whatever that may be. Perhaps it is something you have wanted to do for a long time but it is been sitting on your backburner, the backburner of tomorrow, waiting for the time you feel inspired to dust it off and do something about it.

Maybe someone or something has made you feel inspired to set yourself a new challenge, perhaps something adventurous, get a new career, learn a new language, lose weight, sign up more clients; whatever it is, the idea of it excites you and you intend to take action on it, don't you?

One of the meanings of the word inspired is inhaled, as in inhaled air. Being inspired is just like taking in air, a big deep breath and we can carry on for a little while without taking any more in, but not for long, eventually the air, just like inspiration, runs out and we have to get more. Of course, inspiration of the kind we are talking about will last a lot longer than a breath of air, and how long very much depends on what you do with it. Unfortunately all too often we feel inspired for just a short amount of time, perhaps for a couple of hours or even a few days, after the initial inspiration occurred, but then find that we get distracted by something else or perhaps bogged down with everyday life and the inspiration begins to run out, and before you know it, it is long forgotten and whatever you where inspired to do has also been long forgotten or remains on the backburner, niggling away at the back of your mind.

This all sounds pretty bleak, and possibly very familiar, but all is not lost. I want you to continue to be inspired, I love inspiration, I eat it for breakfast, lunch and dinner, I just want you to do something with the inspiration, I want you to be inspired and I then want you to be committed to the action you are inspired to take.

You need to be committed to action, without commitment there is very little action, if any at all. When you get that flash of inspiration and feel excited about whatever it is you would like to accomplish you need to make a strong commitment to it. "I'll give it a try" or "I hope to make that happen soon" or "when I have time tomorrow" all leave far too much to chance. If the thing you have been inspired to do is not that important to you, then perhaps let it go, however if this is your dreams we are talking about here, no matter how big or small they may seem in the grand scheme of things, they are important to YOU, they are an integral part of you and of who you want to be and how you really want to live your life, then you need to be committed to taking action, so committed that rather than being a dream or wish, it is an intention, this is going to happen and you are committed to making it happen.

So how about not leaving it to chance and making a commitment, a real commitment to achieving your intention to enable you to get the results you know would give you a great sense of achievement? It makes sense that if we are committed we will have a greater chance of getting the best results and making the intention happen. You really do reap what you sow. Imagine your intention is now a reality, because you committed to it and you took committed action to achieve the best possible results. What is that worth to you? What are you prepared to do to make your intention a reality?

When we are committed it means we won't accept anything less from ourselves. It is the difference between waking up and knowing that we are getting up right now, (to exercise/ write that chapter in your book, send out five emails before breakfast for example) we are committed to it and there is no other option, the decision has already been made, it's automatic, as opposed to giving ourselves the choice right then and there as we lie in our warm cosy bed, as that is when the mind battles begin " I really should get up and (insert action) ...or maybe I should just stay in bed, I could give myself a day off, it's really cold, I will do it tomorrow instead and I am feeling pretty tired, oh I know I should get up but I'll just press snooze for 5 more minutes" and we all know how that story ends!

Now you may be thinking that you haven't got time to commit to your intention. You don't have to focus solely on this one thing 24/7 to the detriment of everything else. It means that you do the very best that you can. It involves analysing your lifestyle and looking for ways to make this work. Perhaps you could eliminate some time wasting activities from your life that on the whole don't enrich it. Maybe you need to stop flicking through hours of TV programmes you aren't really interested in and limit your viewing to what you actually enjoy or instead of spending hours each week going food shopping, get it delivered. You can then use that new 'freed up' time to take action on the areas of your life that really are important to you ,those areas that will improve your life, giving it more purpose, direction and excitement. Being committed, as far as I am concerned, mean's giving the best of yourself to something that matters to you. By the way if it matters to someone else, but not so much to you, then either makes it matter or let it go.

In 2010 my life was a mess, I was over 450lbs in weight, I had lost my business and my most important relationship was under threat of coming to an end because of my own self indulgent, self destructive behaviours. I was lucky enough to attend a seminar where I was inspired, I was inspired to make a commitment, and I committed to my partner that in the next 90 days I would lose 90lbs. That's a big ask, but I was committed. I did what we all do, I got on the internet to find a solution to a problem, and I found it in a TV weight loss contest, The Biggest Loser. I got my place in The Biggest Loser, as the heaviest man ever to take part in the UK version, and through a long hard process, I kept focused on my intentions and my commitment. After 24 weeks, I lost 180lbs, more than anyone ever in the UK, and against all the odds, I won. I know, believe me, I know that would never have happened had I not made that commitment that day. Perhaps there is someone you can make a commitment to, and I mean a real commitment from the heart, who will support you, push you and even force you into action if need be. Think now for a minute of who that person might be and what that commitment will be.

To commit fully your intention has to have a real value to you, and you need to understand what that value is. Answer the following questions with total honesty to yourself:

What are you inspired to achieve? What is your core why? On a scale of 1 to 10 how much do you really want this to happen? How will you feel when you accomplish this? Why do you want to do this so much? What difference will it make to your life and the lives of those you care about? How committed are you really, to make this happen, right now as you hold this book, on a scale to 1 to 10 (a clue; the answer is an even number above 9). Who can you make a commitment to? Who will support you? And finally time for action, what can you do now, in the next half hour to take your first step no matter how big or small you think it is ...write it down then go and do it NOW!

Excellent! You have commitment and you have taken action! Pretty simple but so very effective, you are now on your way to your intention. Now you just need to keep that commitment going and create massive momentum. With this is mind decide, right now, the next five things you will commit to doing and five things you can commit to each week to maintain your commitment and to fuel further momentum?

Being committed to what you want to achieve and *why* it is important to you, creates an even greater desire in you to get it, to be even hungrier and yes, even inspired, to do it. You create your own inspiration by realising how important it is to you that you achieve it. By making a commitment to it you are telling yourself that this is something that is now a part of your life, something that has a place in your life and is something that you now choose to spend time on. It has become a priority, not just a dream on your wish list, or a plan on the back burner.

By making your commitments clear you are literally letting your brain know what you want to achieve and why. This will make it easier for you to automatically take actions that bring you closer to your goal, dream or intention. Your brain is there to serve you with your commitment, and you can give it instructions. Your brain will be alert and on the lookout for opportunities to help you succeed, your 'success radar' will be up. Every time you take a step in the direction that you want to go you are programming yourself to keep taking those steps, you will create ingrained positive habits and you will soon find yourself automatically and effortlessly following the desired path towards success.

Every time you accomplish something, whether it is something you consider to be big or small; a step in your journey or the completed task, you set yourself up for further successes. You build momentum, which is extremely powerful and motivational. You begin to see yourself as someone who sees things through to the end. This is empowering and raises your self-belief in your ability to achieve the next challenge you set yourself. You will begin to view yourself as someone who can commit to what they want, take the necessary action and get the results that you set out to achieve.

To help you continue to stay inspired remember to remind yourself along the way why you are doing it, what it means to you, how committed you are and what you have achieved so far. Your commitment then becomes your very own inspiration.

In 2010 Kevin's life was not what he had intended it to be, his life was a mess, through taking responsibility and making a commitment to take action he has turned his life around, winning a TV weight loss contest and establishing himself as an authority in commitment making and action taking. Kevin is an inspirational motivational speaker, mentor and coach. His clients are encouraged to take responsibility, make commitments and take action to release themselves from the things that hold them back from being the best version of themselves they can be.

Contact details

www.kevinmclernon.com

Kevin.mclernon@live.co.uk

Chapter Four
Stop wasting valuable Time.
By Gunhard Keil

"The meeting of personalities is like the contact of chemical substances; if there is a reaction, all are transformed" Carl Jung

Why are so many meetings are boring, inefficient and pointless and how you can change it?

Let's take a look at it from the point of view of various participants. Some typical thoughts that occur depending on their perspective...

An employee: "They've been talking for hours and I don't even know why I'm here... oh well, I'll just check my emails on my BlackBerry...

Another employee: "They've been talking for hours about things that I'll have to deal with later but I can't get a word in edgeways..."

An expert: "Why do they keep interrupting me? There are some really important details that need to be considered which can have an enormous impact on the project..."

Another expert: "Why bother..... no matter what you say, in the end the boss will decide whatever's best for him regardless whether it is sensible or not..:"

Manager: "I can't stand this drivel very much longer... if they don't get to the point soon, I'll just make a decision regardless wether it is the best solution or not..."

If you recognize yourself in one or more of these perspectives, you might find it well worth your while to read the next few paragraphs.

Why meetings can be so awful and what it costs

A few figures to get started: a survey of 1,800 German managers turned out the following results: 68% spend up to 50% (in average 31%) of their time in meetings. According to their estimates only about 41% of meetings or of the time spent in meetings is productive, leaving 59% of unproductive time. The other 32% spend more than 50% (in average 61%) of their time in meetings. The estimates here get even worse: only 21% of these meetings or of the time spent in the meetings is productive, leaving 79% unproductive.

Let's derive a little calculation from these results:

100% of managers spend at least an average of 31% of their time in meetings and believe that 59% of that time is unproductive. If you were responsible for productivity and finances of a company you should be knitting your brow: what it means is that 18% of management resources are being wasted.

It gets worse: the most dissatisfied are the representatives of higher levels of management. They say that they spend an average of 61% of their time in meetings and 76% of them are unhappy with their productivity. The same calculation as above yields that 46% of the time of higher management, the leaders of the company (!), is being wasted.

If you want to feel a little worse, just work out what that can mean in terms of cost for a company....

So what are the typical problems that so often make meetings run this disagreeable course? You have probably already read books that list the 10 don'ts of meetings etc. and I can only confirm that they are probably all true.

If we look a little closer, a few interesting fantasies come to light that contribute to the meeting problem...

The fantasy that the meeting is "only" about the matter at hand

If that were the case, we would simply fill computers with data, program evaluation algorithms and accept the results as the best possible solution. Who would want to work for a company like that? Not I.

Humans are sociable creatures and want to communicate with one another. A horrible experiment at the end of the middle ages illustrated this: Emperor Maximilian wanted to study "natural speech" and ordered newborn infants to be brought up with every available luxury and care, with a single rule: the nurses were not permitted to speak a single word to the children nor to communicate with them with gestures or in any other way. The Emperor hoped that the test children would start speaking the original language of mankind. The poor children all died long before they would have been able to talk.

Humans need relationships and relationships define much more of the content than some would like. The research group around Don D. Jackson, Paul von Watzlawick and Virginia Satir at the MRI in Palo Alto has proven this repeatedly and published their results in a number of books amongst which „Pragmatics of Human Communication: A Study of Interactional Patterns, Pathologies & Paradoxes". Karl Kraus said the same in more humoristic terms, more easily usable in the context of meetings: "Humans must communicate even when it is insignificant".

The fantasy that everyone always has to attend...

It is a common opinion that the more people participate in a meeting the better because it raises levels of identification with the results. That is true enough but in practice it means that invitations are sent out to liberally. It is called the cc effect from the sadly all too common practice of sending emails to as many people as possible via cc.

As mentioned before, relationships play an often underestimated role in meetings: you may have a different estimate how large the open or hidden influence of relationships on meetings is but I am assuming we can agree that relationships need to some extent to be "managed". Do you recognize at least one of the following comments? "We must take care: that is a sore topic for Mr X..." "Please be careful, Mrs Z could take that badly..." "Don't introduce the topic of filling the vacancy: Mr Z and Mrs X are both applying for the post..." etc. etc.

Put it this way: when only 2 people speak to each other, the complexity of the relationship equals 1. When a further person is added, the complexity rises to 3. With 4 people the complexity is at 6 and 5 people are managing 10 different relationships. And that can be incredibly demanding!

The next effect in the chapter "everyone always has to be there" is as follows: if each person were to be given their equal share of time, then in a meeting of one hour and 6 participants, each person would be allowed to speak for 10 minutes and would have to listen for 50 minutes. Some may have more to say than others and some may like to say more but one thing (almost) everyone has in common: they prefer to talk than to listen.

So what often happens at meetings with more than 10 people that last longer than 1.5 hours: asides, email communication, gentle snoozing or sudden, urgent topics being added to the agenda... There is a good enough reason to take the warning seriously: please decide carefully, who really needs to be there.

And because it this about identification with the subject matter and with the results and that identification is more commonly born of doing something together and not of listening, here is another time critical effect best described by the Bavarian comedian Karl Valentin when he said: "It has all been said but not yet by everyone."

The fantasy that there should be a meeting for everything

"...and so I would like to conclude that in future all pencils will be ordered in red and not blue in better compliance with CI!" 12 people nod.

In the course of my research I have often noticed that topics were given inappropriate importance in meetings or that meetings were misused for topics that were not obviously relevant.

There are many reasons for this.

To start with: insufficient perceived appreciation (my topics are important too and I want to have my limelight at this meeting). It is irrelevant whether it is their need to profile themselves or their inferiority complexes that make people want to discuss non-meeting matters in a big circle.

It can also be the control addiction of some big chairman that makes even members of higher management prefer to call up a large meeting, making as many people share the responsibility just in case something goes wrong rather than making decisions independently or with just a minimum of coordination. It is a popular trick to circumvent responsibility by always being able to arm oneself with the excuse that everyone was consulted in advance and gave their approval.

Even though it only takes a little common sense to know who can contribute valuable content and who should therefore be present at the meeting, the non-topic-related effects still play a major role. Once again we see that logic and rational justification are not enough to make a meeting efficient, relevant, result-oriented and fun. Yes, fun. I'll come back to that a little later.

The fantasy that someone who can talk, can communicate

This one amuses me most. The statement "someone who can talk, can communicate" is about as true as saying "someone who can write numbers is a mathematician". Those most in danger of succumbing to this disastrous error are high level experts in recognized fields of expertise.

In my experience so far, the most difficult groups have been people with technical degrees, lawyers and specialized doctors, followed closely by university professors. (If you belong to one of these groups my apologies in advance for the necessarily unfair generalizations! Still, I would be glad of your feedback as to whether in your experience discussions amongst colleagues are not a lot more strenuous than in other groups!)

I can for example prove that in expert discussions the following communication problems occur most frequently: instead of trying to achieve common understanding by collecting facts and creating a collective overview and only then evaluating the issues and initiating the necessary discussions, the participants focus on heated and embittered discussions about details of facts and circumstances that appear to be subject to disagreements. Nobody checks whether the topic is even relevant or whether the discussion serves the greater goal.

Do you know who is served by such discussions? Egos and the competition. Once again we note that the matter at hand is pushed to the background by other, emotional and "human" motives.

The fantasy that knowing how to do something means doing it

How many people do you know who know that smoking is unhealthy and who know how to stop but who still don't stop smoking?

Or the issue with physical exercise: most people know it would be supporting one's health but still we don't do it. In many situations of our life we know what we should do, what would be best for us, the situation, for others involved. But still, we don´t do it.

Once again: I won't bore you with the usual rules for efficient meetings. You probably know them as well as I do. Particularly when it comes to meetings, all you need is commonsense (and to put the inspirations of commonsense into practice) to realize what makes meetings successful, or to be more precise, what could make meetings more successful.

Because to know about something, does not necessarily mean to be able to handle this. I know about Golf but unfortunately I cannot play properly. And even if I knew how to play golf, it does not automatically mean that I am following all rules to be obeyed in order to play correctly.

You have just read a selection of the most prominent reasons why that doesn't happen! Not being used to it, being too lazy and finding good reasons why not to do it are amongst them.

A simple approach to making things better…

"Technology always develops from the primitive, via the complicated, to the simple." (A. de Saint-Exupéry). When it comes to meetings, we have been down this path and I don't want to set up a complicated system (that nobody can use because that is exactly what it is: complicated). I want to give you a few simple tips that should help you avoid the experiences I have described up until now. If you need a more complex solution, I would be happy to help, so don't hesitate to get in touch.

Simple.

Whilst describing the problematic fantasies I kept coming back to a few main pillars or elements that are always at work in meetings:

Relationships. Purpose. Facts. Emotion.

The list starts with relationships for good reasons but you should start your own deliberations with…

…purpose

Ask yourself the first question. What is the purpose you wish to fulfill by calling this meeting? Ultimately there are 4 goals (not reasons why!) that motivate people come to a meeting:

1. Social contact (relationships are back in pole position)
2. Information
3. Development of new solutions

4. Decisions

...and actually, to agree on actions in order to make their own goals, wishes, dreams... reality. Or to put it simply: to create facts.

What does this means for meetings? Just add the ultimate goal of the meeting to the word meeting and you are already inviting to an information meeting, a development meeting or a decision meeting. And not just to a meeting. Taken literally: you will have fulfilled the purpose of a meeting when you have met and the purpose of a discussion when you have spoken.

If you have invited to a "Meeting about the new car policy", then it is sufficient to have exchanged ideas, explained other company policies on the subject, just listened or caught up on your email correspondence, to have fulfilled the purpose of the meeting. What happens if you have invited your colleagues and staff to a "Decision-making meeting on the topic of the new car policy" (a dreaded topic because it is always emotional – not only for male participants) and then you fail to make any decisions? It becomes clear that the assembled team was not able to fulfill the purpose of the meeting.

It is quite simple: Give your meetings the name of their purpose eg. Decision-making meeting for ... and much will change.

Relationships

"I just liked the teacher..." is a common answer if you ask someone why they were good in maths, history or another particular subject. A good relationship is a powerful motivator to focus on a subject.

Co-operation works better when the relationship between people is friendly rather than just topic-related or professional. How do you enter into a relationship? By liking a person, thinking about them... maybe. But more often by going towards the person and exchanging a few words with them. Even just by talking about the weather, you can build a relationship. (Please don't understand that as a recommendation to stock up your repertoire of small talk with a list of weather-related remarks!)

You maybe recall the small matter mentioned earlier of the need to communicate. Now imagine you have called a meeting with an interesting topic. There will be people coming who like each other, people who do not and people who haven't seen each other for a while and just want to catch up but they all have one thing in common: a need for contact.

Use this need for contact and relationship and start your meeting with the agenda item: bilateral exchange of information. You could of course call it check in coffee, warm up round or general meeting over coffee but then many people would only come to the official start and they would still have the need to chat to their neighbor, to ask if they missed anything etc.

That is why it helps if an important person within the company is present at the bilateral exchange of information, at least the first few times. You'll soon notice that the agenda item is particularly appreciated and you might even find it difficult to move onto the more structured part of the meeting.

Our experience shows that this 15 minute investment at the beginning of a long meeting is well worth it since it means that the participants have already established contact and do not need to use the more impersonal topics within the formal framework to make contact. Especially as this can be quite difficult.

When you do start the meeting make…

...the purpose...

...clear again: the „what for" that brings you together. How often have I seen meetings begin with "Today we will be discussing the introduction of a new CRM system..." and that is exactly what happens. They discuss it! But no decisions are made, no responsibilities distributed, nothing written down about who will do what until when... they just talk. Exactly as it was announced in the introduction!

Try to imagine what is going through the mind of a meeting participant when at the beginning of a meeting they are told: "In today's decision-making meeting we will define the functions of the new CRM and the measures necessary for implementation including deadlines and responsibilities." By using this effect called priming you set peoples' expectations to feel that without decisions and the definition of actions, the whole exercise was pointless. Simple, isn't it?

Facts...

... are necessary for decisions. On the one hand to check the plausibility and on the other hand as arguments to convince people about the goals you are trying to reach.

But how do you get the relevant facts? Usually there are more than one clever heads around the table that could and should provide facts, whether from marketing, sales, legal, production, engineering or personnel. Experts are an important source of information but not everything is relevant to every topic. The art is to work with the intelligence, the creativity and the knowledge of other people to get exactly the information necessary for decision making and piece it together to a complete picture.

That means using the collective intelligence of the group. We have run various simulations that prove that statistically speaking the collective intelligence of a group is better than an individual intelligence. To this effect we asked a group of people to make a ranking of priorities on the basis of incomplete information, first individually, and then to discuss the ranking in the group and deliver it as a result of a consensus within the group. A correct ranking by priority was only possible with the collective information of the group. The individual results differed according to the person's capacity to work with partial information.

Between 1994 and now the result in 90% of the simulations studied have delivered the same qualitative results:

- The mathematical average in more than 90% of the cases was better than the best individual result.

- Depending on the maturity of the co-operation within the group, the result of the discussion was worse or better than the mathematical average.
- The most important weak point was the commitment of the group to the result. The participants usually didn't feel that the result of the discussion was right but that their own result was the correct one (which of course contradicts the idea of "CON-SENSUS") So they often stayed with their original result and by that did not go for the better ranking from the group.

In short: the challenge is not only to collect existing information but to create a concordant, lasting, common picture, where everybody feels committed and aligned to go for it. But isn't that the final purpose of meetings? Beneficially working with the knowledge and the talents of all the people involved, getting a focus on what has to be achieved?

What helps? The three rules of discussion:

1. Collect information first, before evaluating
2. Look for points of agreement before addressing differences
3. First create an overview before collecting details

Emotion - joy

What most meeting initiators or decision makers want, is the commitment of the meeting participants to the decisions made and to their subsequent implementation.

Here is a question: how do you bring commitment into the factual context?

Commitment is an emotional quality in reference to a topic. To give an example: if someone sees the following fact as correct: "it is necessary to cancel a holiday and to continue working in order to achieve a project result" but is not committed to the goal, to the action and/or to the company, they are more likely to make their decision in favour of their holiday than in favour of the company's interests.

Someone who believes that they can generate commitment and emotional attachment by simple rationality is making a particularly fatal mistake: that of intellectual arrogance. This can turn up in various forms such as so called corporate visions expressed uniquely in terms of turnover and profit. The fact that this represents nothing but a dangerous threat for most employees, is something that the "visionaries" oversee (to an attentive employee "Our vision for 20xx is to double our turnover and at the same time double our profitability" only means:

work twice as much and twice as fast for the same wages and is therefore nothing but a threat). Joy is not the most frequent reaction to such statements.

Back to joy and to meetings. There is a phenomenon that I continue to find interesting: a large proportion of meeting participants do not feel the most emotional quality when working in a professional, structured ambiente where personal interests are put in the background. On the contrary, they enjoy free, unstructured debates and discussions and the less binding the discussion and the more optional, the more fun it is.

To carry the same idea further: given that the genuine function of meetings is to inform, create new possibilities and finally initiate actions to reach goals, we have to find a solution where both elements, ratio and emotion, have their place.

Repression of any upcoming feeling does not work, so make sure there is room for it, especially if you are expecting a lot of emotional reactions, no matter whether good or bad.

And on the other hand: an enactment of feelings is also not a very promising strategy. I have never experienced, that a person trusted another because it was written in the mission statement (we trust in each other, we cooperate professionally and so on)

The best way is to plan app. 25% of the meeting time for emotional issues. Some might find that contradictory to what is written in the beginning and the estimation of how much time is spent productively. Depending on the agenda of the meeting you might not need this time, but let me assure you, most probably you will, reasons for that please see above.

And the proposition is: if you expect a lot of controversial and polarising energy, plan it in at the beginning of the meeting. Actually you should provoke it to be articulated. Then the emotional cleansing effect takes place before you start with the fact-oriented discussion.

If you expect positive reactions, take some time at the end of the meeting, enjoy the success you had and see the 10-15 minutes when you are having fun as a very valuable, motivating and commitment-founding investment.

Summary of how to be significantly more successful in meetings in 5 Ps

People meet people and work with people. Give them 15 minutes time to get in contact and make it a standard in your meetings, called: bilateral information update

Participants: please select carefully who you invite to participate in the meeting

Purpose: name your meetings with the genuine purpose they serve – decision meeting, information meeting and so on.

Process of discussions:

1. Collect information first before evaluating
2. Look for points of agreement before addressing differences
3. First create an overview before collecting details

Pursue the agreements you made unconditionally, set up the action plan and execute

A few last words... I hope you enjoyed reading this short outline on meetings. If you are thinking of changing your meeting culture and transforming it into a more efficient and joyful one, the return on investment will be tremendous. I wish you lots of success!

Appendix: All the know-how and experience I have cumulated in the last 20 years have been the basis for a supporting shareware solution called "*tact*". *tact* paces the process of preparing a meeting, conducting a purposeful meeting, creating action-oriented minutes and tracking the outcome of a meeting.

Gunhard Keil, entrepreneur, top executive coach, consultant, arbitrator and speaker is an expert on performance management, diagnostics and meeting excellence. Many international corporations have taken profit from his 25 years of experience on how to manage meetings efficiently, working with the creativity and potentials of your staff and unleashing the energy that makes a difference for all, customers, employees and shareholders.

He is founding member of 5p Consulting, CEO of Syntegra Consulting and has put his expertise in a unique software solution called "tact" to prepare and direct meetings efficiently, come to decisions and track tasks.

Gunhard is a renowned speaker for meeting efficiency, conflict management and how to find the right person for the right job.

Besides that he is engaged in social work, being the vice president of the Sanitary Corps of the Knights of Malta, Austria, in pursue to help people with special needs.

Contact Details:

Gunhard.keil@5p-consulting.com

www.5p-consulting.com

www.tactyourmeeting.com

Chapter Five
How to speak your truth and reap the rewards
By Tonya Joy Bolton

"The most revolutionary act one can engage in is... to tell the truth." By Howard Zinn

How to speak your truth and reap the rewards

Speaking our truth is a subject that we can all relate to, regardless of race or *culture*.

We live in a world in which we're encouraged to pretend that everything is great, even when it's not for many of us, myself included. *Despite it being a vital ingredient to living a fulfilled and authentic life,* it's actually much easier to talk about speaking our truth than it is to actually do it.

Speaking our truth isn't always easy is it?

Most of us spend our lives in constant fear of other people's possible reactions if we were to say what we really wanted to say. Much of the time these fears keep us in a state of silence and powerlessness.

So many times, we keep our thoughts to ourselves in order to save someone else's feelings or in order to avoid judgement and rejection. How many times have you failed to speak up when you disagree with your business partner or bit your tongue in a business meeting? How often have you not listened to your intuition and kept quiet to avoid creating conflict with your clients or colleagues?

So what do we believe will happen if we tell our truth?

- People won't like us
- We will be judged
- People will think that we don't like them
- We will hurt people's feelings
- People will know the 'reality' of our situation
- We will have to deal with a confrontation
- People will disagree with us
- We will inconvenience people
- People will be totally honest in return
- We will be rejected
- We will lose our jobs

The list of options and possible outcomes goes on and on.

We often think that keeping quiet is the easy option. But is it? We often don't stop to consider what the benefits are of telling our truth.

Make no mistake, speaking your truth is risky business and you won't often win any popularity contests, but the personal sacrifice to withholding your truth is even greater.

It's painful and we *may not be aware of the damage it is doing to us on the inside, especially in our bodies.*

You walk around **worrying you'll say the wrong thing.** You're often seen and not heard. You regret biting your tongue and **kick yourself for days** when you miss your opportunity. You hold things in until you've developed a stomach ulcer and by the time you finally speak up you explode! This is obviously is not the best way to end up with a win-win solution to a conflict.

Most of us grow up learning how to relate to each other mask-to-mask, instead of heart-to-heart. I'll be honest I used to be someone who preferred to stay silent, but my silence was literally killing me. As an Empowerment expert, I'd spent years constructing a facade of "perfection" around myself. I was a high achiever and good at looking happy. There was certainly a lot to love about my life. But i also lived with a lot of anxiety and fear.

I didn't want anyone to know that i had once suffered from depression, I didn't want anyone to know that i had been raped. i didn't want anyone to know I'd once attempted suicide...shhhhhhh!

I believed that I was a 'strong' woman, a 'professional' person and a 'good' girl. Those kinds of things don't and should never happen to people like me! Like so many of us I blamed myself and the guilt and shame crippled me.

But when I discovered that an alarming number of Black and Asian women were not reporting sexual and domestic abuse in Birmingham or accessing sexual health provisions I felt an overwhelming sense of responsibility to stand up and speak my truth. In doing so I found strength I never knew I had.

So i wrote a play and performed it in front of a packed sell out theatre knowing i was about to tackle some very taboo issues. It was in fact the first time in Birmingham that the issue of sexual violence within the Black & Asian communities was discussed in such an open forum.

I didn't know what to expect but thank God when the play ended I didn't have to go into hiding and my world didn't end. The opposite happened. Not only did I get a standing ovation from every single member of the audience, it changed my life, and also the lives of others.

My courage to "speak our truth," inspired and empowered others to do the same. I can't tell you how many people have shared their stories with me. Sometimes I am the first person who has heard the story. It's an incredible privilege to be let into someone else's life in such an intimate way. I now regularly receive letters and emails from courageous men and women sharing stuff they've repressed for years-Someone walked away from an abusive marriage, someone started writing their autobiography, someone changed careers and decided to follow their dream of pursuing a singing career, someone came out and accepted them self as a homosexual. The list goes on...

Speaking my truth was the greatest *gift i could have given myself and my community.* In speaking my truth, I reaped and still am reaping massive rewards!!! It turned out to be the best thing that ever happened to me professionally and personally. My career skyrocketed and my personal power increased. My willingness to be vulnerable, and to reveal my own personal story, helped catapult the play to break box office records and i am now organising a national UK tour as we speak.

I now attract more clients because my clients know I will tell them the truth about their businesses. Corporate sponsors pay me to be a spokesperson for their companies and I get invited to be the keynote speaker at conferences because I speak my truth on stage. I now get paid to speak my truth, and it feels AMAZING!!! Not only do I no longer have knots in my stomach and lumps in my throat from keeping my mouth shut; I also get rewarded for speaking my truth!

What I have learned personally about the power of speaking your truth is that it can actually be the golden ticket to your success and if harnessed wisely will get you ahead in your career. But speaking your truth pays off in so many other ways too.

Speaking your truth is a very powerful experience. You'll discover benefits that will literally transform your life for the better!!! By speaking your truth you will grow stronger and discover a whole new kind of **self-confidence**. Not only will it liberate you, but it has the potential to make a difference for others and bring us closer together with them. It can **build trust and respect.** It can resolve conflicts and deepen existing relationships while attracting new ones. You'll discover new ways to communicate with clients as well as loved ones. You'll experience the joy of **living in alignment with your authentic self** – every day for the rest of your life.

People often focus on the negative outcomes of speaking the truth but interestingly when you *deliver your truth* with integrity and compassion; **hard-to-hear information** is actually refreshing and impactful. It **makes you powerful** simply by being yourself.

Although the thought of speaking your truth can feel so scary at times, **it will not kill you!** in fact you have a greater chance of dying if you don't speak your truth. Medical research show that when we don't tell the truth or avoid the truth we begin to feel the effects by a tightening in our chest as well as other physical symptoms that happen in the body. Over a long period of time these can turn into more serious physical conditions.

Ultimately, for me, speaking my truth wasn't just an important part of my healing. It led to powerful discussions through which others solved some challenges they'd been facing, uncovered and resolved others that we hadn't even been aware of and came up with ideas for new ways of doing things which benefitted them as a whole community. If I hadn't shared the truth about my experience, those conversations would never have taken place. So I ask you...where in your life do you need to speak your truth? ...and what could it possibly uncover that wouldn't be revealed without it?

Clearly you need to overcome your fears in order to speak up and reap the rewards. But if you're unsure about how or when to speak your truth, and stuck in the fear of what might go wrong when you do, you're not alone! Here are some tips I learned along the way on How to increase the likelihood of reaping the rewards from speaking your truth.

Key 1: Know Your Truth

Your truth is who you really are at the core of your being. It is who you are without the pressures of family, society, religion telling you who to be. Most of us have built up layers of pretence over the years to protect us. Letting go of this false self is the gateway that opens you up to knowing your truth

In order to reveal that self, we need to find stillness and silence for a dedicated period of time on a daily basis. During this time, its useful to reflect on how you were taught "truth." Were you encouraged to deny or ignore your personal truth? Many have been taught that speaking the truth was wrong or rude and offensive to others, so you became a people pleaser in order to keep the peace and not hurt feelings.

What is your truth? Are you suppressing your real truth? For instance have you ever wanted to be a painter, but you became a lawyer because you felt it was the better career for you? if so, then you are suppressing your truth.

Of course, this is a simple example, and our truth is about more than our professional calling. It is about the choices we make every day. Sometimes our truth says that we need to leave a relationship or move house. Are you taking the time to listen to your inner truth?

Key 2: Speak Your Truth

- **What does it mean to speak your truth?** Once you have systems in place to help you recognize your truth, the next step is to be able to effectively honour and communicate it. **Don't bite your tongue anymore or let them ignore you.** Speak up effectively. Maintain your integrity in *every* situation and **be true to yourself**. Every time you feel yourself hesitating to speak remember that your voice is necessary. What you have to say is just as valuable as everyone else's! You have a right to be heard.

- **Free yourself from the need to be right:** In order to speak your truth you need to be fully connected to what's in your own heart. When we let go of our attachment to the outcome of a conversation, what the other person thinks, and our obsession with always having to be right, we give ourselves the opportunity to get real and grow. Truth is not about being right, it's about expressing what we think and feel in an authentic, vulnerable, and transparent way. We need to let go of being "right" about our opinions and take responsibility for our experience. Only then can we speak our truth from a much deeper and more authentic place. The next time you are in a conversation, take a moment to check in and see what's truly in your heart and begin to communicate from that place.

- **Speaking your truth is not a box of chocolates.** It can be incredibly challenging and scary. Like anything and everything else in life – the best way for us to get better, deepen our capacity, and grow, is to practice so give yourself permission to take time to build up your courage and get clear. Will you mess it up? Of course! Will you say the wrong thing sometimes? Yes. Will people get upset, offended, or defensive at times? Absolutely. This isn't about being perfect, it's about being yourself and speaking authentically. Have empathy and compassion with yourself as you practice. You may be uncomfortable so practice speaking your truth every day. As time goes by it will feel more natural.

- **Become aware :** Notice around whom or in what circumstances you tend to withhold the Truth. Begin to notice who triggers you to keep your mouth closed or hesitate. In order to begin speaking your truth, it's important to start noticing when you aren't being yourself, and begin to free yourself from the dependence on positive reactions from other people. Just noticing where and when we shut down is the start of changing the pattern.

- **Have no attachment to the outcome:** Your Truth is subjective and may not be anyone else's truth. However, what you have to say is still of great value! It deserves to be spoken and heard. We can't control someone else's perception or manage other people's feelings, but we can give our truth a voice. Before you begin to speak, let go of your attachment to any outcome and know that speaking your truth is enough.

- **Respect:** Speaking your truth is not all about getting up in people's faces and being aggressive. You don't have to be hurtful to speak your truth. In fact whenever you speak with anger - frustration, confusion, separation and regret are your end results. Speaking your truth requires compassion, wisdom and tactfulness. You'll be amazed at the capacity people have to hear the truth when it's communicated from your heart.

Key 3: Live your truth

- To live in your truth is to be in integrity with yourself. If we don't do this, we betray ourselves, and that is the worst kind of betrayal. We have to be completely honest with ourselves, and this requires courage. It means hearing the answers you don't want to hear. Living your truth means *taking off the masks we wear. It means we stop worrying what others think of you and refusing to pretend to be anyone you are not. It means being honest with ourselves and other, finding strength in that honesty and having those tough conversations*

- Living in your truth means accepting and embracing all aspects of who you are. Since you are the *only* version of you ever to walk the planet, trying to live someone else's life is impossible.

- When faced with a tough decision, ask yourself what is my highest good in this moment? What is the best action for me to take? This will give you clarity and create balance.

I want to conclude by asking you some questions:

What if you had the courage to speak up in all areas of life – your work, your relationships, and your family?

What if you were to say exactly what is true for you from your heart and soul?

What if you were to say what is true for you without sarcasm, anger, impatience, or fear of judgment?

What if you were totally real, totally YOU in your relationships and career?

The answer is that you would find your personal power, experience peace, drop resentments, and let go of all the conversations you are having in your head of frustration with yourself or with others.

Imagine the freedom and power you would possess. *So what's stopping you?*

Sadly I know so many people who have died and taken their extra-ordinary truths with them to the grave.

The benefits of speaking your truth far outweigh the payoffs you get by remaining dishonest with yourself and others. If you decide that you are too afraid to speak your truth, you will remain stuck, sick, and trapped in a prison of your own making.

If we don't speak our truths how can the next generation learn?

Not speaking your truth not only dis-empowers you and robs you of your mental, emotional and physical health, but ultimately your silence does a disservice to your community and the world.

When we speak our truth we become leaders of our own lives, we drive change, realise dreams, transform lives, we heal others and ourselves. If you want to reap massive rewards than **I urge you to break your silence and speak your truth by:**

1. **Being fearless.**
2. **Being honest.**
3. **Being transparent.**
4. **Being unapologetic.**
5. **Being you.**
6. **Believe that what you have to say & do matters**
7. **Believe that you matter**
8. **Make sure it's coming from your heart and not your ego**
9. **And finally know that when you speak your truth, you and the whole world benefits.**

Tonya Joy Bolton is a multi-talented empowerment expert for young people and women. She is also an international speaker, writer and performer. As the founder of ICU Transformational Arts Limited and The Woman Arise Institute, Tonya has over 12 year's experience of working with vulnerable people who have poor emotional and mental health, and social difficulties. She has a proven track record of successfully raising aspirations and attainment while reducing the likelihood of risky behaviour, such as self-harm & eating disorders.

In 2012 Tonya spoke about sexual violence at the first ever TEDxBrum event and recently completed a sold-out tour of her powerful and deeply moving play 'Holy & Horny.' Ultimately Tonya is passionate about using the arts to help people break destructive cycles and move forward into the life they want and deserve. "Tonya Joy Bolton is not only breaking box office records but helping to change lives." The Voice Newspaper, October 2012

Contact details:

Website: www.icu-transformational-arts.com

Email: tonya@icu-transformational-arts.com

Chapter Six
Leadership – Creating an Inclusive Vibe around You
By Charlotte Sweeney

'Every Person Influences Culture - take responsibility for the part you play and be an authentic and inclusive leader'

Whether you're an executive in a firm or an entrepreneur with your own business you're a leader. You're a leader of business, a leader of people and a leader of yourself.

Being a leader by default means that you are at the forefront, taking the helm, for others to follow. But, are you a leader that others want to follow? Are you a leader that, in a world of increasing globalization, considers cultural differences and flexes your style to really get the best out of the people around you? Do you adapt and change so that you can engage your clients on their level and build a respectful and productive relationship? If you do, you certainly have the makings of being an inclusive leader.

But what do we mean by being an inclusive leader?

Before we get into the detail, let me take you back in time to think about your career and the leaders you have encountered.

Can you remember a time when you were led by someone who listened to your ideas, encouraged your input, acted on the suggestions you made, constructively challenged where appropriate, made you feel like a valuable member of the team and made you want to go the extra mile?

You can? What else did the leader actually do to make you feel like that? How productive were you while working with that person?

Think back again, can you remember another leader that made you feel valued and important? A leader that made you want to push through to the next level, lit a fire in you that made you want to be able to inspire people just as they had inspired you, supported you to become the best you possibly could be, encouraging you to go the extra mile...and you wanted to deliver the best product or the best service for them?

Again, how did that time in your life feel? What else did they do to make you feel that way? What did they motivate you to do that you may never have done without them?

Now lets come back to the present day. Thinking about the experiences you have had in the past can you imagine being that leader? The one that others look up to, the one that others speak about just as you have with your experiences, the one that encourages them to be their best and will go the extra mile for?

If you have never experienced working with a leader like the ones mentioned above (and some people truly haven't) can you imagine being that leader? Imagine what you could deliver if you had a team around you that were inspired and motivated to be the best they could be, what level of service would your clients experience and how would it feel knowing you had inspired and encouraged that level of performance?

Being a leader isn't purely about what you deliver and the targets you achieve...its about understanding how you make someone feel. People around you may forget what you say but they will never forget how you make them feel!

You could say that the examples mentioned above are just really good leadership skills. They are! But how often do you actually see them in action?

This is what inclusive leadership is all about.

Being an inclusive leader is understanding how someone ticks, understanding how to get the best out of them, treating them with respect, valuing their contribution, being interested in them as a person and supporting and encouraging them to be the best they possibly can be.

So What?

So, why is all this important? It's important for a lot of reasons...all of the reasons are important to consider if you are an executive or an entrepreneur...or someone who is committed to their personal success in an ever-changing world!

It will come as no surprise that the business landscape is changing rapidly. The development of the knowledge economy is seeing a flatter, less hierarchical structure in organisations. Technology is enabling companies and entrepreneurs to 'do business differently', trades take place across continents in a matter of seconds, millions of emails and text messages fly around the world every single day, social media platforms influence both company and personal brands and the traditional 9 to 5 is slowly becoming a thing of the past.

The world demographics are also changing. Over 56% of first degrees in the UK are obtained by women, more than 10% of the UK workforce is from an ethnic minority background and 6% of first class honor degrees are gained by students known to have a disability. We are coming into an era where there will be more people over the age of 65 than there are under the age of 18 and people will want to continue working past their normal retirement ages for both personal and financial reasons. This means that we can expect to see more generations in the work place all with their individual needs, expectations and aspirations...as well as expecting them to work together effectively.

The above is just a sample from the UK. There are similar pictures across the developed world. What impact will this have on your business, the people you hire and the people already in your team? What impact will it have on your clients?

Regardless of what business or sector you're in...a large multi-national delivering products and services on a global scale or a small to medium sized business focused in one country all of these issues will have an impact on your business. You could well be leading people from all walks of life and getting the absolute best out of all of them will be critical.

So, how do you do that?

By being an inclusive leader and creating an inclusive vibe around you and your business.

The qualities and characteristics of an inclusive leader

So, what are the next steps of becoming an inclusive leader? Or, if you already lead your people in this way, how do you hone your skills? There are a number of qualities that inclusive leaders, be they executives or entrepreneurs, display. These can be broken down further covering what they know, what they do and how they do it.

The core qualities of inclusive leaders:

- **Being Adaptable**

Inclusive leaders are highly aware of the diversity amongst the people they work with and the people they do business with. This 'diversity' can range from background and experiences, ages, genders, thought styles and many other differences that make up each individual. They are comfortable with using different and flexible approaches to truly get the best results from their teams and deliver the best for their clients. They are skilled at adapting their style to complement others and do this in an authentic way.

- **Championing Innovation**

Inclusive leaders understand and value the small, incremental innovations that can improve quality, productivity, client satisfaction and cut costs as well as larger scale innovations that can result in new products and markets. They embrace the philosophy of 'Kaizen' and believe that continuous improvement and 'change for the better' is a given business practice. They are skilled at creating a working environment that encourages and fosters innovation, an environment where all involved feel safe, valued and empowered to innovate.

- **Skilled at Finding Great People**

Inclusive leaders understand and embrace their role and responsibility in seeking out and supporting the development of great people. They actively look in different places from their competitors for these great people and leave no stone unturned, where-ever it may be, to find and support those with potential.

These qualities may have already started you thinking about what you already do, what you should start doing and what you can do differently. Breaking this down a little more into the characteristics of inclusive leaders by looking at what they know, what they do and how they do it will support your thinking further.

- **What they Know**

1. Inclusive leaders know that to get the best out of their team they should have a varied range of skills, knowledge, experience and backgrounds. They should also know how each individual contributes to the wider team knowing their background and the unique strength they bring.

2. Inclusive leaders know that they must develop their ability to flex their own personal style to engage and get the best out of those around them. They are emotionally intelligent and know that this is about

adapting their style appropriately rather than completely changing their style.

3. They know that creating a culture of two-way communication is vital for their team and business success. They know that this is also critical in creating successful and sustainable client relationships.

4. Inclusive leaders know that we all make assumptions about people and situations. Although these assumptions can also be characterised as 'going with our gut instinct' and can serve us well they also know that reflecting on those assumptions and the decisions made using them is a wise and educated move. Taking a couple of minutes out to sense check the situation and validate the decision made is a good business move and minimizes the impact of assumptions that may not serve you well.

5. They have the ability to build and create a safe environment that empowers creativity, innovation and problem solving. They encourage people to try new things, to do things differently and know how to discuss situations that just don't go to plan.

6. Inclusive leaders are skilled at finding out what the personal motivators and drivers are of those in their team. They actively find ways to leverage this information to maximize individual and team performance. They take this one step further and actively find out what the motivators and drivers are of their clients, delivering against them where possible to build stronger relationships.

- **What they Do**

1. Inclusive leaders get to know the people in their business personally. They know what makes each individual 'tick' and ensure they ask about their lives outside of work on a regular basis.

2. They focus on the quality of the work delivered by individuals and the team rather than the hours put in. In other words, they are output focused. They encourage people to work flexibly and push them to organise their work in a way that suits their own individual style throughout their day.

3. Inclusive leaders help those around them understand the strategic bigger picture of what they are focused on

achieving and help the individual understand how they fit into that picture.

4. They help others around them identify their own strengths, encouraging them to build on those and use the skills to the best of their ability. They acknowledge their areas for development and support where necessary, however, the focus is firmly placed on strengths. They know that not everyone needs to be good at everything in a diverse team with many different skills and strengths.

5. Inclusive leaders actively seek out the ones that could make it to the next level and could do more. They support their development and growth and push them to make the most of themselves. They help individuals to find new opportunities to hone and promote their skills.

6. Inclusive leaders are open to feedback on their performance, behaviours and their skills. They are eager to listen to any form of feedback regardless of the level or position of the person offering it.

- **How they do it**

1. Inclusive leaders trust other people to do the right thing in all situations and believe that the best intentions are always the key driver. They know that people are trustworthy and honest and see that as the default setting.

2. They are approachable and really do demonstrate a genuine interest in others. They want to know more about the people they do business with, both team members and clients, and genuinely start with the default setting of respecting people from the beginning of the relationship.

3. Inclusive leaders are authentic. They do what they say, they act as they speak and are consistent with that. What you see is what you get!

4. They are open about their own strengths and weaknesses and happy to discuss these if they believe it will support individuals or the wider team in some way. They know when they are the best person for the job and when it should be handed over to someone else with different skills and strengths from their own.

5. Inclusive leaders are resilient. They constantly go the extra mile and will constructively challenge behaviours in themselves and others that do not place respecting people at the heart of them. They will not accept inappropriate or bullying behaviour in their business.

6. Inclusive leaders want the very best for others and will support them in their personal career and business goals.

How many of the above points can you say, hand on heart, that you display on a regular basis. If you were to ask your team and the people around you what would their response be? Would it be the same, or very different, to your response?

Does it really matter? Is all this important for business?

In a nutshell....Yes, it really matters!

In an increasingly competitive world you should want your business to be the 'go to' place for your clients and deliver the very best with the resources that are available to you....those resources also include your people! People want to work for and do business with people they like and make them feel good. In the grand scheme of things being an inclusive employer doesn't cost anything. It's a mindset....that can have a significantly positive impact on your business bottom line!

A Few Questions to ask Yourself – Are You an Inclusive Leader?

1. Do you know the different values and drivers of the people that work with you? Do you use this information to motivate them and help to improve performance?

2. Do you sponsor and champion people, from all backgrounds, with high potential to support them in realising their career aspirations?

3. Do you ask those you manage or lead for feedback on the impact of your style or approach in supporting them to perform well? Have you ever thought about asking a client about the impact of your style on them? Could this support the relationship in some way?

4. Do you challenge others if they display behaviours or actions that are inappropriate and do not support the mindset of being an inclusive leader?

5. Do you help those around you understand the bigger organisational and strategic picture and articulate their role within that?

6. Are you aware of the stereotypes, assumptions and judgments you make about different people? Do you sense check your decisions to minimize the potential negative impact of these? Do you encourage others to do the same?

7. Do you involve and encourage those you work with to identify challenges early on, come up with solutions and ways to improve the business and what the business does?

8. Do you actively look for people from different backgrounds and experiences to bring an alternative perspective to your business? Do you encourage their involvement and leverage this to avoid groupthink?

How did you do?

Are you an inclusive leader? Are you getting the best out of your people and your business? Are you creating the relationships with your clients that will take your company to the next level?

Charlotte Sweeney is an executive leadership coach, consultant, mediator, international speaker and conference facilitator. She has specialised in large scale change programmes with a focus on diversity, inclusion, engagement and wellbeing for over 15 years and has delivered these for global companies. She is also seen as a thought leader in her field, regularly developing and creating new research and works with companies and executives from the private, public and third sectors across a number of countries to support leadership and cultural change. Charlotte believes that every person influences culture and creates strategies and programmes to bring that to a reality with the organisations she works with.

Charlotte is also a board member for a number of not for profit organisations and sits on numerous advisory panels for governments and local authorities. Over the years she has won many awards, both in the UK and globally, for the progress she has made in this field and for her personal commitment.

Contact Details

Email – charlotte.sweeney@sky.com

Website – www.charlottesweeney.com

Chapter Seven
Give Youth A Chance
By Peter Knight

"A youth is to be regarded with respect. How do we know that their future will not be equal to our present?" *Confucius.*

Why your business should include young people in its recruitment strategy

Is your business missing out or at a disadvantage because you don't include young people in your recruitment strategy?

Are you sceptical of the value of youth employment? Placing undue emphasis on experience and neglecting the opportunity to attract and develop raw talent that can be trained in your company's way of doing things? Are you bypassing hungry young people, who bring with them a willingness to learn, enthusiasm, fresh perspectives, flexibility and up-to-date knowledge, thinking and skills to name but a few of the benefits?

If the answer to any of these questions is yes then you are not alone. A 2012 survey by the Chartered Institute of Personnel and Development ((CIPD) Learning to Work:

Survey Report) found that three in ten employers in the private and voluntary sectors (one in four in the public sector) did not recruit a single person aged 16-24 in the 12 months prior to the September 2012 report. Looking ahead, only 58% of private sector employers (52% public sector and 46% voluntary sector) expected to recruit young people within the next twelve months.

So, if there are so many benefits, why aren't more businesses recruiting young people? There are a number of reasons. Many employers are nervous about employing them because of negative perceptions about their attitude. Some are unconvinced of the benefits of employing them because they don't believe that they will have the necessary skills for the business. Others are just 'out of the habit' or have a, perhaps unjustified, preference for graduates or someone who can 'hit the ground running'. For some employers it is simply the case that they do not have jobs that are suitable for the employment of young people and, understandably, no employer is going to recruit a young person for whom they have no use. I believe that the latter category is a distinct minority as the young can do most things.

It is absolutely vital that the current trend away from the recruitment of young people is reversed if we are to avoid our youth becoming what Bell and Blanchflower (2010) called 'the lost generation'.

Recruiting young people is good for business, good for the young and good for society.

The following is an analysis of the perceptions and attitudes of business, the benefits young people can bring to your organisation and the ways in which your company can become more engaged with and employ the young.

Please note that throughout this work the term 'youth' is used to refer to young people in the 16-24 age range.

Employer perceptions and attitudes towards young people

Research conducted by the CIPD in 2012 (The Business Case for Employer Investment in Young People) found that employers have the following perceptions and attitudes towards the employment of the young:

1. **Attitude**

   Many employers are 'petrified' about employing young people, because of negative perceptions about their attitude.

2. Benefits/Risk

Managers are unsure about the benefits of employing a young person and see them as a 'risk'. This was supported by a British Chambers of Commerce survey in 2011 (The Workforce Survey: Micro Businesses) that found that almost half of the employers interviewed are 'fairly' or 'very' nervous that a school leaver with A-levels or the equivalent would have the necessary skills for their business.

3. HR Professionals are 'out of the habit'

HR professionals have got 'out of the habit' of recruiting young people and, as a result, they 'don't ask the right questions' and 'don't know how to recruit young people and how to talk to young people'. For example HR professionals would ask young people about their work history, when they have never worked.

4. Managers have 'lost the skill to manage young people'

Managers have 'lost the skill to manage young people' and they worry about the level of pastoral care they need to provide.

5. Preference for graduates

Employers ask for graduates, even if the job doesn't require graduate qualifications and they don't offer as many entry level jobs as they used to.

6. Preference for somebody who can 'hit the ground running'

Employers prefer to recruit somebody who can 'hit the ground running' rather than investing in nurturing and developing the young.

In addition, a report produced by the CIPD in 2012 (Learning to Work: Survey Report) found that:

Nearly half of employers (47%) agree that young people are disadvantaged in today's labour market. They also believe that young people need an opportunity to prove themselves.

Some employers express concerns about young people's readiness for work, with 59% agreeing they have unrealistic expectations about work, and 63% agreeing they lack insight into the working world. In all, 57% of respondents agree young people lack work experience and 53% think they lack adequate careers guidance. Almost half of the respondents say young people are not prepared for work.

However, among HR professionals that had recruited young people in the last 12 months, satisfaction levels were generally high. In all 91% of employers were either very satisfied (26%) or fairly satisfied (65%) with the young people that they had recruited. Just 9% of respondents were fairly or very unsatisfied.

Almost a quarter of the employers surveyed said that an increase in the quality of applications from young people would encourage them to recruit the young and a similar proportion cited help with funding from the government.

A further 22% reported that a greater assurance that the education system is delivering more job-ready young people would encourage them to recruit from this age group.

I acknowledge that the perceptions and attitudes above are limited to those identified in one survey. However, this is merely intended to illustrate that the perceptions and attitudes that exist may be irrational.

The benefits to business of employing young people

Numerous surveys and reports (including those named so far) have identified the benefits of recruiting and employing young people. These include the following:

1. Lower recruitment costs

Young people in school and college tend to be actively seeking employment and many apply speculatively directly to employers saving you the costs of advertising.

By engaging with schools and colleges your business can gain access to good quality recruits whilst cultivating a reputation for offering jobs to young people which will encourage others to apply – particularly if you are known for providing good training opportunities. This will widen the pool of applicants from which you can draw.

2. Cost effective

Younger workers don't demand the salaries of more senior employees, making them a more cost effective choice. Also, where employees are under 21 years of age, a lower National Minimum Wage rate applies.

3. Flexibility

Young people can often be more flexible in terms of the hours that they are prepared to work as they lack the ties (e.g. children at school) that older employees have. They tend to be more adventurous and, as a result, willing to be more mobile in terms of the geographical location in which they are prepared to work.

Young people are also flexible in terms of valuing the opportunity to get involved in a variety of tasks, allowing you to meet the changing needs of your business.

4. A willingness to learn

Young people are more willing to learn, not burdened by previous ways of doing things nor set in their ways.

5. Qualifications

The expansion of further and higher education intakes means that young people represent the highest qualified age group of potential recruits ever.

6. Up-to-date knowledge, thinking and skills

Through their very recent education and interest in technology (smart phones, tablets, MP3 players, games consoles, computers etc.) young people bring with them the most up-to-date knowledge, thinking and skills;

7. Shared organisational culture

Young people come into organisations with no preconceptions providing employers with the opportunity to instill their organisational values and to 'shape' employees to fit their way of working.

8. Insights and connections into the market

Dependent on the nature of the business, young people can provide important links to the customer base. They are current consumers and future (if not present) purchasers of goods and services. They can bring important insights into markets, especially those that change rapidly or are subject to fashion such as music, computer games, clothing, footwear etc. where young customers dominate the market.

9. Staff retention

Investing in young people, either through offering a first job or through training, can enhance loyalty and reduce staff turnover. This, in turn, helps maintain productivity and reduces future recruitment costs.

10. Innovation and energy

Young people may bring new ideas or knowledge into the business. This may be particularly so if they have come directly from university or college or where they have been engaged in off the job training.

11. Succession planning

Recruiting young people allows the organisation to plan for the replacement of older staff that will be retiring in the future. Recruiting young people who can grow and develop into viable internal succession candidates that know and understand the business can reduce the risks associated with unplanned retirements and potential staff and skills shortages that would otherwise need to be met by external recruitment at additional cost.

12. Diversity of perspectives and experience

Having a range of ages in the workplace brings diversity, mutual learning between colleagues and a good balance of experience and fresh ideas to the organisation.

13. Aspirations and valuing work

Young people value work and the benefits that it can bring. They share the same aspirations as their older counterparts to pay their way in society and to have a car, home and a family eventually. They desire the feeling of independence and do not want to be reliant on their parents. They also aspire to the self-esteem that developing in a job brings. I have witnessed these desires and aspirations personally in talking to a number of young people when exhibiting at recruitment fairs. These young people are far from the stereotypical apathetic and unmotivated unemployed on the contrary, they were highly motivated, eager and optimistic in their search for work.

How your business can invest in young people

It is acknowledged that the business case for recruiting young people will vary depending on the current situation of each individual company and that not all organisations will have jobs that are suitable. However, many businesses, both big and small, could benefit from making far better use of the talent pool that is youth. The following are some of the ways in which you can do this:

1. **Create an internship or apprenticeship position;**

    An internship or apprenticeship can be a flexible and cost-effective way for your business to recruit a new employee. The position can be paid or unpaid depending on the role and provide the business an excellent opportunity to assess the new employee.

2. **Offer a Work Trial**

    A Work Trial is a way of trying out a potential employee before offering them a job. Once agreed with Jobcentre Plus, you can offer a Work Trial if the job is for 16 hours or more a week and lasting at least 13 weeks.

3. Use the Graduate Talent Pool

The Graduate Talent Pool is a free service which allows you to advertise your live internship opportunities to new and recent graduates.

Organisations of any size from the public, private or voluntary sectors can advertise internships on the Graduate Talent Pool. Most of the internships advertised are based in England, although employers from other parts of the UK are welcome to post vacancies on the site.

Graduates can only apply for vacancies if they graduated in 2010, 2011 or 2012 from a UK university with at least a degree or foundation degree.

4. Use a Knowledge Transfer Partnership (KTP)

Knowledge Transfer Partnerships (KTP) is a UK-wide programme enabling businesses to improve their competitiveness, productivity and performance.

A KTP achieves this through the forming of a Partnership between your business and an academic institution (such as a university, further education college or research and technology organisation), enabling you to access skills and expertise to help your business develop.

The knowledge sought is embedded into the business from the knowledge base through a project, or projects, undertaken by a recently qualified person (known as the Associate), recruited to specifically work on that project. KTPs can vary in length from 6 months to three years, depending on the needs of the business and the desired outcomes.

5. Engage with Schools

Your organisation must engage with local schools by making staff available to visit them free of charge to:

a. Provide an insight into the types of jobs that exist – to help students to consider their career options;

b. Highlight local career opportunities i.e. provide details of current and future vacancies; and

c. Provide insights into recruitment such as effective application, covering letter and CV writing and interview technique (including mock interviews) etc.

Not only are you helping schools and young people in doing this but it is also an excellent PR opportunity for your business as you can publicise what you are doing via local media etc.

Start engaging by contacting your local schools today. This must form an integral part of your Corporate Social Responsibility (CSR) programme.

Summary

Youth unemployment has been high and rising since before the recession and continues to. Other factors are clearly having an influence not least a reluctance on the part of business to recruit from this pool of raw talent. This may be due to negative perceptions and attitudes about young people, to a lack of appreciation as to the benefits of their employment, to a lack of awareness of the best way to employ a young person or a mixture of these.

Employer perceptions and attitudes, such as those identified above, are open to challenge:

There is no denying that reservations about attitude may be valid where some young people are concerned. I would argue that the majority are positive in their outlook and are keen to work, to pay their way in society, to grow and develop as individuals and to boost their self-esteem. This has certainly been my experience in meeting young people at recruitment fairs.

Yes, there is a risk inherent in employing a young person but isn't there a risk in employing anybody? I can cite many examples from my own experience of cases where older, experienced people have been recruited to the organisation with high expectation but have failed to perform.

If HR professionals are out of the habit of recruiting the young then they need to get back into it and quickly for the benefit not only of the young but of their organisations.

A good manager should have the ability to manage people of all ages and be equally skilled at managing the young as well as the older, more experienced employees.

When recruiting we need to question whether a graduate is really necessary for the job or whether a school or college leaver would be adequate. In recruiting for a junior accounts position recently I received CVs from a range of candidates from school leavers, to the unemployed and graduates. I was particularly drawn to that of a school leaver who had worked his way up from being a delivery driver with a well-known pizza chain to Assistant Branch Manager. I was less interested in his qualifications and more impressed by his ability to advance his career, which was clearly due in large measure to his attitude and motivation – valuable assets in any employee wouldn't you agree?

Sometimes business needs dictate that a candidate must be able to hit the ground running but each case should be judged on its merits and the young not ruled out where there is time to nurture and develop their talent.

Whatever the reason, the perceptions of business must change, business and schools must work together in partnership to better equip and prepare the young for the labour market and the young themselves must work diligently on their own marketability.

It is not just about providing employment to young people (although it is a big part of it) but generally engaging with schools and the young. Visiting schools to provide insight into career opportunities and recruitment such as effective CV writing and interview technique (including mock interviews) etc.

For their part schools need to better equip their student's for the labour market by helping them to improve their application, CV and interview skills – this could be achieved by proactively engaging with business for the delivery. They also need to provide good quality career guidance – something which students, teachers and employers alike tell me is presently lacking. In short, schools need to deliver more job-ready young people to encourage employers to recruit from this age group. It is all very well equipping students with academic skills but their value is diminished without the ability to put them into practice in the workplace.

And, of course, the government has a vital part to play in reducing youth unemployment, through its policies and initiatives.

The tangible benefits of employing young people are numerous and there are a number of ways of doing so. Young people represent a rich pool of raw, enthusiastic, motivated and flexible talent that can be trained in your culture and work practices and become long-serving, loyal employees whose cost-effectiveness is beyond doubt. This is the reason why your business should include young people in its recruitment strategy.

Your business has nothing to lose in employing young people and, potentially, everything to gain.

Give youth a chance!

Peter Knight, a qualified accountant and MBA with more than 20 years senior financial management experience, founded Your Career – Mentor in August 2012.

Its aim is to help young people to find and pursue their ideal career, linked to their passion, so that they live happy, fulfilled lives and reach their full potential. In short, the objective is to help them to make "their choice for tomorrow today" (a play on the title of Peter's forthcoming coming book).

Peter is a personal performance and youth impact coach, public speaker and presenter of regular workshops for young people.

Peter, a former senior manager with Kumon, is passionate about helping young people to reach their full potential.

Your Career – Mentor is proud to be a member and supporter of Youth Employment UK – which aims to increase the number of young people in employment in the UK.

Contact Details

http://www.yourcareer-mentor.com/

peter.knight@yourcareer-mentor.com

Chapter Eight

Life's a Pitch... and then you buy
by Steve Clarke

"Whatever business you're in, you're in the business of sales. "- Steve Clarke

Now for some people that will make your toes curl - the whole idea of being in sales - making a "pitch"... might fill you with fear and dread.

You may even be tempted to skip this chapter now - don't...

If being in sales leaves you cold, you'll find all the excuses under the sun to get 'busy' and avoid picking up the phone or making that all important presentation.

But here's a fact - no sales, no business. You could end up with a hobby - and a very expensive one at that.

If you are serious about having a successful business or key position within a business today – It's vital that you stand out from the crowd... (for the right reasons).

It's imperative you learn how to deliver winning presentations, written or spoken. To succeed you must discover the secrets that allow you to communicate effectively face to face, one to one or a thousand and one and even to an invisible audience... via email, sales letters or a web site.

In this chapter I'm going to give you three simple tips - that if you implement them, they're guaranteed to help you stand out from the crowd and win business... so please read on...

Having achieved a degree of success in my own business career, I'm privileged to now spend my time helping other business owners - perhaps just like you, discover how, with the right attitude, and with the right actions, you too can have the life and business others just dream of.

Let this book be your instruction manual... That's what we were asked to create. A handbook for busy executive or entrepreneur.

Ok, how many of you actually read instruction manuals?

I know some people that read them cover to cover, follow every instruction to the letter meticulously.

Some people are capable of speed reading... accurately, others speed read recklessly.

Perhaps, like me, you'd prefer to read in chunks. Take a little time to digest... and dip back in for more food for thought - or should that be thought for food... whatever.

It doesn't matter what your reading style is - as Nike would say... "Just Do It".

Whatever great advice you get from me or anyone else - without the right activity, which you test and measure, you could be in danger of just getting busy.

Don't confuse busy with productivity.

"Vision without action is a daydream, action without a vision is a nightmare!"

There are sections in this book designed to have you pause and think about how certain ideas and concepts could be applied to your own situation - don't restrict yourself to this... feel free to highlight key points that resinate with you, scribble in the margins too if you like - it's your book. Make it a working copy.

But here's the funny thing.

Even with the exact same instruction book - people will get very different results. I'd really like to hear how you get on. What I know about is how you can get your phone... and in turn... your cash registers ringing...more enquires, more leads, more clients, more sales... more profits.

I wonder - what will you choose to do with all this information?

Before we go any further - are you up for a challenge?

Yes? Seriously...? OK then read on...

Why do some people succeed where others fail?

Its a big question, but I firmly believe there aren't in fact too many answers.

All the successful people I know have made a decision to create the life and the business they want. The rest, (many of them great people, so don't get me wrong)... take what comes their way, they go with the flow, they accept that things just happen to them.

But here's what I see. The doers, the achievers, the people I see having extraordinary success in their lives and their businesses – take control. They're in the driver's seat, they have the steering wheel firmly in hand, they take control, responsibility and they take action!

What of the others? They take the role of the "victim". There are always reasons why things don't come their way, why they don't get the orders, why the cash flows… (but always the wrong way).

Here are three things I've observed from people that say they want to succeed in business and in life, but often… why they fail to meet their goals.

1. *Blame*. They will always find someone or something to blame on the lack of sales, lack of profits or lack of success. They'll blame the government, the economy, their competitors, anyone but themselves.

2. *Justify*. They will usually attempt to justify that things are ok. They'll say things like… "well, it's not all about the money, it's not that important". Take that attitude and it wont be with you for long if ever at all. Imagine saying the same about your husband or wife, they'll not be around for long either!

3. *Complain.* Complainers attract crap like a magnet! Sorry, but it's true. It's proven time and time again that you attract what you focus on. Complain and moan about everything and things will only get worse.

So - here's my first tip for success.

I'd like to offer you a challenge right here, right now. Ready...

Here it is... For the next seven days – no complaining.

Whoa... tough one.

Not about work, not about clients, not about kids, partners, traffic - nothing... no complaining.

Will you take the challenge?

I think you'll be blown away with the massive changes it can deliver too. Go on – I dare you...

Think about it, what good does complaining and focusing on bad stuff do to you? If you focus on crap what are you going to get?

Crap!

So stop being a crap magnet!

Crap doesn't travel at the speed of light - it travels at the speed of crap and it just clings on for ever.

Let's face it were creatures of habit, right?

Yet we're not born with the habits, we learn them.

Monkey see, monkey... do. We've all heard that too, well we're not so far removed from the monkey are we? We learn our responses to circumstances and situations, so it figures we can learn different patterns too and not just take what comes out way.

Just like robots, we get programmed a particular way, with certain patterns and behaviors. You can paint the robot so it looks great, looks new, but the programming is just the same and so the results will be too.

What stops people from achieving the level of success of others and changing their programming, their believes and behaviors to reach new heights?

Fear. Fear of the unknown, fear of failure, fear of uncertainty. It's what stops people picking up the phone and calling a hot prospect, making that all important pitch etc etc.

So are successful people fearless? No, not at all. But they take action in spite of fear!

We are controlled by our thoughts which produce feelings, our feelings translate into action and the action we take delivers results. Simple.

If your thoughts of business growth or success fill you with fear and dread, feelings of potential failure or uncertainty and doubt, how powerful do you suppose the actions you take will be?

You don't need to look at the results you're getting now as the best results you can achieve. Instead, consider your results as the fruit on a tree. You can't change the fruit once it's there, that's too late.

If you want to see change, if you want different results look to the roots, that's where you need to make changes. That's why we call it the "root cause". Cause and… effect. Change the roots you can change the effect, and the results...

What are you going to focus on and think about? Good stuff or bad, problems or solutions? What you focus on affects how you'll feel. How you feel will determine the action you'll take and the results you'll get the fruit on your tree.

Once you take decisive action in pursuit of your goals, the fear melts away and confidence grows.

Now stop complaining… let's see the results you want and deserve.

What will you choose to do with this information?

Here's another secret for success.

For those of you that want to see a positive "step change" in your results don't go it alone.

You should consider joining a mentoring or master mind group. Seriously, the awesome power of a like minded master mind group must not be underestimated.

Knowing that others are hitting the same walls, facing similar challenges as you - but finding solutions they're willing to share - fantastic!

Having a positive peer group that will lift you up on those tough days... Amazing!

A coach and a mentor to hold you accountable for your actions or inactivity - this is powerful stuff.

Whilst I'm a successful sales and marketing coach and mentor myself, I currently have two mentors and my own coach helping drive me forwards with my own business - who's helping you?

"I always looked forward to my monthly injection of enthusiasm from Steve and the Mentoring Group. I am so excited to be part of the Platinum Master Minders - we see results and reap the rewards week after week!"
Denise Stoker - Leo Print.

Valuable tip number 3 - dare to be different.

"It ain't what you do... it's the way that you do it... that's what gets results." Bananarama

The times I've heard people say;

"Yep, tried that it doesn't work."

"Yep, that's fine for them, but that wont work in my business."

Rubbish!

Vishal Patel had tried direct mail - it didn't work. He'd given it up as a bad job.

Outdated marketing strategy, direct mail doesn't work any more, that was his conclusion.

Yet applying the Bananarama concept, "it ain't what you do it's the way that you do it", to direct mail produced fantastic results for Leicestershire based Vishal.

He was open to new ideas, are you?

Having heard me speak at a business event in London, Vishal decided to travel south again a few weeks later to attend one of my "Turbo Charge Your Sales" seminars.

With his permission, here's an extract from an email mail he sent me soon after attending;

"A few months ago we were listening to Steve as he told us about a direct mailing strategy that we had never used before. I'd tried direct mail, but never got any worthwhile results and could easily have dismissed the idea of mailing ever again.

However, we decided to try mailing using one of Steve's new ideas. We put it to use straight away and the results were absolutely amazing!

Using this one bit of advice and applying it to our sales letters over a 2 month period got us 4 new contracts each worth a net £4,000 - over £16,000 from a direct mail piece and more in the pipeline."

Vishal Patel, The Directorate Corporation Ltd.

Within the pages of this book there are nuggets of pure gold.

Select the elements in the book that click with you and get cracking.

You might have to "Pan" for gold. Some concepts might require a little polish, a wash and brush up, before they're pure gems for you - but they're in here I promise.

Pick out the pieces that look right for you and your business, see the results others have achieved and decide if that's what you'd like to see for your business.

It's all about attitude - and action.

I live by my mantra "It's your attitude that determines your altitude".

Do I have off days? Yes. But I know how to regain my focus, do you?

In business and in life, attitudes are infectious – make sure you're spreading something good!

You can moan and groan, bitch and whine – it will do no good! Will it help you reach your goal? No.

If you are to succeed in business, if you are to win more sales and make more profit – it's down to you to make things happen. It's been proven time and time again that with the right "mindset" ordinary people can achieve extra ordinary results.

How do you frame success and failure in your mind?

How specifically do you view failure?

Inventor Sir James Dyson doesn't believe failure "sucks"... (get it?...sorry). He says;

"I made 5,127 prototypes of my vacuum before I got it right. There were 5,126 failures. But I learned from each one. That's how I came up with a   solution. So I don't mind failure."

I know so many people with tremendous potential that simply never get out of the starting blocks due to their limiting beliefs and fear of failure, don't fall into that trap.

Crack on!

Steve Clarke

Sales and Marketing Mentor, Author, Inspirational Business Speaker...

Steve left school at the age of 16 with no qualifications, direction or purpose in his life. At 19, with a fresh attitude and determination to succeed, he found his niche in sales. Shortly thereafter he was invited to become a director of his first company.

Since then he has owned and operated businesses in the UK and USA. He has taken them from start up to stock market flotation.

He grew his last UK business from scratch to £30m in annual revenues in just 8 years, sold out and retired at the age of 45.

Now, in addition to running his Sales Mentoring and Mastermind Programs, he delivers sales training to leading companies around the world, lectures at Universities and is regularly engaged as a keynote inspirational business speaker internationally.

Steve's mantra... "Your attitude that determines your altitude".

Contact Steve Clarke at:

steve@eurekasales.co.uk

www.eurekasales.co.uk

Chapter Nine
When Two Worlds Collide
By Richie Maddock & Anne Garrod

"Much like earths relationship with the universe, people are realising that today's business world is increasingly interconnected - If our values and behaviours influence our individual worlds, is the world of your business aligned with that of your customers thereby avoiding a galactic near miss? "

Is this a Star Trek fan writing this? How can organisational values and culture be linked to what happens in space? The truth is it probably can't, but something happened recently that got us thinking about the relationship between an organisations workplace culture and the values of their customers. On February 15th 2013, Asteroid 2012 DA14 passed within 17200 miles of our planet. According to the experts, this is deemed as 'close'. The event raised many questions of intrigue amongst us earthlings and in particular what would happen if it was nearer or changed course suddenly and headed for the planet? As one would expect there was a lot of theoretical information banded about but there was an admission in some quarters that in reality there wasn't much research to answer the question in practical terms. Some said it would be a waste of money researching something if we cannot prove a significant risk of real danger – but it was only after researchers started looking that they realised just how many 'near earth objects' there are. Now we know they are out there, what are we going to do to protect ourselves?

We had fallen into the trap of thinking that if the risk of a truly disastrous event is small, unknown or just too complex and difficult to think about, we can discount how bad things would get if it occurred and not waste time and resources into trying to grasp a firm understanding of it.

This takes us to the link to organisational culture. As the banking world moves from one crisis to another, as the food inspection authorities scrabble around looking for horsemeat in products on supermarket shelves, there is many a pundit preaching a very simple statement: *The culture of the industry has to change, and change dramatically if their customers are to have any trust in them in future.* More noticeable is how long they have been saying it and yet things appear to remain the same.

Is the subject of organisational culture providing the same trap we had fallen into with near earth objects? Are customers the asteroids hovering around you and who might one day just change course and contribute to a catastrophic disaster for your business. More importantly - are businesses putting time, effort and resources into understanding and managing their culture?

In most businesses and organisations, values statements can be found on walls, computer screensavers and, if no expense has been spared, even mouse mats and pens. These statements lay out a set of expectations the business has of itself and others. They state was is important to the organisation whilst delivering their products or services to their customers.

The company values are a commitment to a set of core beliefs and behaviours and these collectively make up the culture of the organisation and the workplace. Or do they?

From our work on cultural development with organisations we have found few who really understand the prevailing culture of their business – potentially a huge risk strategy with significant consequences, but the risk is unknown and the subject is too complex or difficult to get to grips with – and so follows that very little time or resource is put into really understanding the culture and if it needs to change – until its' too late that is.

Now we know that nearly every business wonders what their customers are saying about them and focuses resources on good customer service and seeking to achieve the ultimate customer experience. You are extremely fortunate if your customer's personal values closely align with yours. If they do then you have nothing to worry about and you are sure to benefit from what they say to others and your relationship with them.

If their values are different however, and they normally are, then the impact of what they say is potentially a disaster waiting to happen.

If for arguments sake, one of your company values is to provide exceptional quality your price will probably reflect it. If your customers don't value quality and care only about cost though, in their minds you're too high-priced for what you deliver and will go elsewhere. Your company values are immediately put into a compromising position.

If another of your stated values, on the wall in the corridor for all employees to see, is treating people with respect and dignity, but you then allow your customers to abuse your employees, or at least have a different level of tolerance because you think you need the business, how can your customer service staff see you as anything but hypocritical?

When your sales team is instructed or even incentivised to meet their quotas no matter what, but that same values statement on the wall says you value relationships, how well will they be treating your customers when a bonus is on offer? Therein lays the conundrum of organisational values and culture. It is more about what is done than what is said.

We were at an Institute of Customer Service conference many years ago, where a keynote speaker was an Australian by the name of Steve Simpson. He was there to talk about a concept he had created to help organisations understand and manage their culture and its simplicity has resonated with us ever since. Steve believed that an organisations culture can be simply put as 'This is the way we do things around here' and the things that are done he calls 'Unwritten Ground Rules – or UGRs®. By understanding an employees perception of 'this is the way we do things around here', we can begin to understand the reality behind the values poster. UGRSs® drive behaviours in the workplace and as humans those behaviours influence others – including the customers' perception of your business. The intriguing thing is that UGRs® take place continually but are rarely talked about openly.

We conducted an exercise with a DIY company recently, where we asked customer service trainers and front line staff to design a training course for their customers – to make them the best customers they possibly could be. After a lot of fun deliberating they settled on some key areas they thought that would help their business and their staff if only customers were more knowledgeable about them. Suggestions ranged from helping them to understand that the store closes at 8pm so it isn't worth arriving at 7.55pm if they wish to enjoy a good browse around the shop floor, to helping them realise that they should not expect every single member of staff to have knowledge on every product available.

They were actually discussing customer expectations and what they value from a good business - and the gap that exists between those expectations and the culture of the organisation. They had no difficulty however in designing the training course which indicated the significant gaps!

The values statement on the wall clearly stated that *'our customers are at the heart of what we do'* but the UGR® in play was 'around here when it comes to being available for customers we have to finish at 8 to get the shutters down and get home' or 'around here we have to put our more junior staff in front of the customers as the senior ones are busy doing other things that head office want sorting'

In this 30 minute exercise the values statement on the wall and the true behaviours became apparent. More importantly, the values statement was visible for all customers to see and their interpretation of what they read will come together with what their own values and expectations are telling them.

If you're wondering whether your existing customers share your values, ask your customer service and sales representatives and your receptionist how they are treated by those customers and whether they see values alignment with what you have on the wall. This conversation is made even more powerful if the member of staff you are talking to believes those values to be real and that they really are 'the way things are done around here'

If a customer however, should ever ask you to change your product or service, or behave in a way that is contrary to your values it takes a lot of strength to stand firm. The decision you make in this instance will determine your prevailing culture.

A bad customer or partner organisation shouldn't be kept on any more than a bad employee who treats your values with contempt. They both undermine your performance, sustainability and reputation. Such actions then become part of your culture and it will become very hard to draw back from that position – as the banking sector is now discovering.

Having a full understanding of how your values statement is enacted by your workforce and having an appreciation of the values that drive customers may mean that you lose some immediate business, but here's what you gain - longer-term customer relationships built on understanding, trust and respect, increased innovation and product/service improvements from an alignment of both employees and customer values and improved dialogue, an increased competitive position from greater stability and reputation and a positive workplace culture within your organisation that is built upon what is done and not just what is said.

In the increasingly interconnected landscape of the business world, where the culture of an organisation is so inter-related with the personal values of customers and partner organisations, it is important that leaders have a full understanding of what really sits behind those values statements when they develop them. Executives need to move from a position of knowing that culture is important and hoping that it will take care of itself to one of having a clear understanding of it, how and what influences it and by whom.

A business is made up of an unimaginable number of those unwritten ground rules that are contributing to business success and performance on a daily basis - and it will require time and resources to fully appreciate them so leaders can take the necessary actions to turn the negative UGRs® taking place into positive ones.

Understanding the values of your customers is equally as important and will not come from a simple customer satisfaction questionnaire. It will need some serious and imaginative effort to gain that understanding.

It is incumbent on leaders and executives to ensure that when the asteroid that is the customer enters the world of their business – every possible effort has been gone into dealing with culture so that they can proactively avoid the collision that will create a significant ripple across their universe.

Richie and Anne are directors of Lynchpin and Associates and specialise in workplace culture and improving the customer experience. Having worked in both private and public sectors, they have over 60 years experience in customer service and organisational development between them and have helped organisations develop their workplace culture to bring company values to life for both employees and customers alike.

Contact Details:

www.lynchpinandassoc.com

Richie@lynchpinandassoc.com

Chapter Ten
Balance Your Mind
By Tony Walker

"Balance your mind to increase your productivity!" – Tony Walker

In every single decision and every living moment we are each in tune to the universe and self to varying degrees. If our lives are the music then our various emotive states are the notes that are plucked by everyone and everything if we so choose. Let us all strive to be conductors of our own lives and use Balance Your Mind techniques to guide.

BALANCE

One definition is this – "A state in which opposing forces harmonise"

In many eyes balance is simply standing on your own two feet or heads! Or physiologically not being swayed from pillar to post in what you say or do. Bio-mechanically balance tells us we have a fully functioning balancing system in our bodies if we are not constantly losing balance and falling over. Even falling over would only pass us off as mentally unstable or drunks.

What if you have no feet, legs or ears and your physiological balance mechanism is dysfunctional? I suggest you can be the most balanced person without these attributes. I am reminded of Nicholas "Nick" Vujicic a Serbian Australian evangelist born with tetra-amelia syndrome, a rare disorder characterized by the absence of all four limbs. But he lives life without limits.

It is clear then that BALANCE is not merely a physical attribute. It is something that we are all born with but may not know how to utilise. It makes up the core of our beings as a human and can be learned and developed by continual practice and never say die can do attitude towards all we do.

Balance and spirituality often go together but one does not depend on the other to exist.

OUR MINDS

If you consider our minds are the beginning and end of the worlds in which we exist. If one loses his mind then one loses his world. We use this faculty consciously and unconsciously in making all kinds of decisions and prior to undertaking all kinds of action. We must remember that inaction or indecision is a consequence of what is or has happened in the mind.

A mind whether balanced or not is not for everyone. But consider this; the world is in the mind which would mean the mind is made up of connected worlds. Each world is then a projection of an individual's mind. Taken further this would mean that the world is made up of connected minds.

The connected minds theory is really another way of saying connected people. When this is at the heart of a business and people pay for a service whatever it may be, that business will thrive and be both productive and profitable. The modern day Social media platforms are based on these phenomena. The next big business trend will be built around these principles.

It's just a matter of what is created in our minds to take advantage of this. The more connected and balanced we are the more productive we are capable of being. The more productive we can be the more profitable we can be also.

BALANCING YOUR MIND

We are living in an enlightened and empowered age where business and spirituality are inextricably linked. Achieving a balanced mind is part of an individual's journey of transformation. The mind gym can be entered into on a daily basis when moving towards balance. It is essential if you want a win win outcome in every situation. When you till the ground and sow the seeds of abundance then the fruit will come.

A balanced Director engenders a balanced Company. Balance brings trust from others and gives the perception that you are conscious in all your undertakings.

Balance may at first seem to come from ourselves. Yet it will not be sustained by oneself. Stormy seas will come in our minds along with dream stealers difficulties will surface and threaten to de-rail you.

The source you connect to and the things you believe in whether you have faith or not will anchor or balance you in the rough waters.

MIND FITNESS

Balancing your mind in action is really fitness for the mind and finding the space at home or in the market place to carry through the practice. It involves bringing your complete attention to the present experience on a moment to moment basis and acting on the divine answer given to you.

In general speak others may say listen to your heart. In essence all your faculties, your whole being and soul are used. You ingest by way of the atmosphere via your senses all available energies, physical and nonphysical to come to a set of possibilities for moving forward or just deciding. In any case this process widens your choice and makes it clear which path you are destined to follow or remain on.

OUR SIXTH SENSE

What is this? Does it even exist? It's all baloney? Yet varying experiences may denounce this other sense and call it something else. The question would still then remain that if you denounce one thing it must mean you believe in something else. Whatever that may be. This on its own points to your sixth sense, though we are blissfully unaware and many of us do not know it is there.

Whether this phenomenon is believed or not it is undeniably a force mightier than gravity to be reckoned with. Even not using this gift is by default using it.

You basically swallow every opportunity using our physiological systems and our whole being and our sixth sense tells us whether it is right or wrong or just not an option to consider at this moment.

You may call it by some other name, however using the ecology of our human bodies, our spirit and the earth – the correct action for this present moment is created unconsciously. This applies to any decision for another, ourselves, an organisation or facilitating Executive and leadership decisions. This attribute is like a muscle the more you use it the stronger and quicker you can call on this ability and process for whatever it is you want answers to.

PRODUCTIVITY AND PROFIT INCREASES

Incorporating balancing of the mind techniques is essential to long-term modern day business success. Training your mind to be balanced makes you more productive

As with many diverse aspects of human nature it may be that A Balanced Mind or not is just used as a tool to enhance a business plan.

One business measure of success may be monetary profit. Another may say it's the number of volunteers giving freely to the advancement of an organisations aims and objectives, whether a Social Enterprise, CIC, LTD Company or a charitable body. Increased productivity and therefore profit will have a positive value to various organisations in different ways.

The cost savings at the 2012 in London is a great example. Many volunteers were used and each person was aware of the Olympic ethos.

SUMMARY

Balance of mind and body of any kind is not desired by all yet if pursued is refreshingly contagious and holistic in nature. If you do choose this path there are many doors towards it. Hear the Sages of the ages and take note of all our teachers in the guise of Sufis, angels, prophets, religion, arts, Science and many more.

The philanthropists of our age by their actions of giving have at least travelled the journey in life to know that holding onto anything is futile. It is in this awakening of letting go that their productivity and profits in business increase.

The universal laws incorporating the laws of attraction and mindfulness are essential ingredients for a super profitable business. There is an awakening in the universe that contributes to an ecology of self that imbues balance and is a pre requisite for spirituality.

Undertake your business with balance in mind and you will succeed beyond your s.m.a.r.t.est plans.

Bound by many universal truths and laws, one being the law of attraction. Yet it is the Balancing of our minds and the personal transformation inherent in this that binds our personal growth with increases productivity. By the power of, whatever number you choose, the potential profit increase is only bound by limits imposed within your mind.

Tony is a Health & Wellness coach and NLP practitioner with over 15 years of specialising in Change and Project Management.

Tony works with a variety of people and organisations from prisoners to vice presidents, small businesses to larger companies such as Sony and Unilever.

Tony has a unique ability to shift transitioning individuals, teams and organisations from their current state to where they want to be. Through his hands on approach, Tony has helped people embrace changes in their business environment and personal lives whether it be achieving weight loss, coping with redundancy or increasing productivity.

Tony is also an international athlete who has competed all over the world and trained extensively in martial arts; receiving many awards in recognition of his achievements. He now teaches people of all backgrounds how to stay calm in a crisis and rise above any situation, and how to let go and free oneself from the limiting beliefs that keep us prisoners.

Contact details

Tony@tonyawalker.co.uk

www.tonyawalker.co.uk

Chapter Eleven
The Value of Values
By Rose Aghdemi

"The glue that holds all relationships together -- including the relationship between the leader and the led is trust, and trust is based on integrity." *Brian Tracy*

"If people like you they'll listen to you, but if they trust you they'll do business with you." *Zig Ziglar*

The value of your values lies in the living, the doing, and the implementing of your values. Only then do they have a positive impact on you, your team and your clients.

Developing a value-led approach to your work, team and individual performance will add enormously to your worth. Carry out your work and achieve results with skill as well as respect and integrity, and you will be trusted and admired. The relationships you build around you (and it's all about relationships!) will then be solid and difficult to replace, as you, your team and organisation become known for working not only with the highest skills but also with the highest values.

In business, the relationship is king

In business, the relationship is king, and if you build unique and special relationships with your clients based on important values then you will stand out from the crowd. When your values such as trust, respect and integrity are incorporated into the relationships with your clients, then this unique relationship will become your point of differentiation.

Let me explain....

If you are dealing with a client based on your product or your price, you can be competitive. But if the client can buy a similar product or service cheaper, they will. If all I need is to arrange to service my car, then I will get it done wherever I can find the quality I want at the best price.

If you offer additional services you will be more noticeable to the client, but even this approach means you are seen as a commodity. Price matters, and you are readily replaceable by a cheaper or more novel option. So I may choose to get my car serviced by a garage which advertises that they offer to collect my car from my home or office and return it after the service is completed. But again, I can choose to buy from whoever supplies that service at the best price.

However - high quality relationships in business are of incalculable value. They are rare, and therefore memorable. They offer that all-important point of differentiation. Let's say I see that a garage which can service my car and offers to collect and return the car, also offers to discuss options for polishing out a scratch on the bodywork. The options include recommendations to external specialists, so do not necessarily mean they will get the work. When they carry out the service they are prompt and the price is as quoted – they are reliable. Furthermore, they tell me I can call them any time for advice on the car if I ever have concerns. They will say when the work is out of their expertise. I trust them to tell me what may be required, whether they will get the work or not. I trust they will have my interests in mind. They may alert me to other services, such as good car insurance deals, which I may like to know about, with no obligation and no profit to themselves. The likelihood is, I will give more business to this garage, with which I now have a high-quality relationship. They demonstrate a value-led business, working with trust, reliability and fairness. If this garage were to change hands, and the staff no longer offered this relationship-based business to their customers, then they would no longer be differentiated from many other garages in my area and it is unlikely that I would feel drawn to continue to give them my business.

> Remember that trust minimises risk for the client and saves them time

When you work by living and demonstrating your values to clients, you will draw others to you because you are trustworthy and reliable. People who have personal and professional integrity can be depended on to behave according to their principles even when no one is watching. Remember that trust minimises risk for the client and saves them time (and time is money!), and when they trust you they will seek you out.

When the client – because of your value and your values - seeks you out, rather than you approaching them for work, the dynamics between you are far more positive. Instead of you justifying your fee, your presence and taking up their time, you are collaborating together on shared aims. You are communicating as partners. So the more you can do to encourage clients to initiate working together the better. Invest time and effort into making sure that your name, your values, your talents and the high quality of your working relationships are known to as wide a range of potential clients as possible.

The most valuable clients to acquire are those with

whom you will have a long-standing relationship with repeat business – ideally over many years. It is difficult to acquire new clients, so it makes sense to nurture your contact with new and existing clients in order to build up high-quality, trusting relationships, reflecting your values, to increase the likelihood of these clients becoming long-standing clients who supply you with ongoing and repeat business, as well as recommending you to others.

Clients are more likely to engage you when a trusting relationship is in place

Clients are more likely to engage you when a trusting relationship is in place. It takes time and patience to build up such a relationship, and it really is a case of taking one step at a time. Think of it as a process of achieving small 'Yes' steps, by which I mean offering options or services which allow the client to say 'Yes' to you when less is at stake. Over time, all these small 'Yes' steps will build up so that you are closer to your goal of doing more substantial business with the client. Remember - it is easier to pursue and achieve these small 'Yes' steps over time than it is to close a large contract in one fell swoop. It takes time and patience, but these will often be well rewarded. The all-important high-quality relationship, based on trust, will have time to develop. The trust is not only based on trust in your word and reliability, but is also based on the belief that you have the client's best interests in mind and that you will act accordingly.

How to build a high-quality, value-led relationship with clients

---

I've explained why living your values is valuable, especially as the key to your success is in developing high quality, value-led relationships with your clients. I turn now to outlining how you can form such relationships, which will reflect your values of trust, respect and integrity:

- Provide more information than required, if it is of real value to your client
- Be available to key clients by giving them the most efficient contact details eg your mobile number.
- Be responsive – aim to return calls and emails within a certain time limit eg 90 minutes for a telephone call, half a day for emails.
- Recommend trusted professionals when they could help your client
- Be tactful but frank. You will help your client more, and earn more respect, by pointing out problems and solutions rather than being an agreeable 'yes-man'

- Treat your client as a partner – you both have a common aim in addressing his or her business needs in the best possible way
- Go the extra mile - it will make a difference. Remember your priority is to build relationships, not merely to provide a service.

Working with values 'inside-out' and 'outside-in'

So far I have been mainly referring to the value of values when working 'from the inside out', that is, reflecting your values through your behaviours and relationships with clients. It is equally important to live your values 'from the outside in', by which I mean ensuring that you attend to yourself, and to your own colleagues, team and organization. Take a hard look at how others see you and your team. Are you known for working with your values? If your five main clients were asked about the values you live with and which your team embodies, would they know what they are? If not, how can you change the way you are doing things so that there is no doubt at all about the values you hold as a value-led team or organisation?

Defining your values

If you are to incorporate your values into living your personal and professional life, you need to know what they are! Your values are traits or qualities that you consider worthwhile. They represent your highest priorities and deeply held driving forces.

What are your values?

Take a look at the suggestions below to see which resonate with you:

Trust, integrity, respect, ambition, competency, individuality, equality, service, responsibility, accuracy, dedication, diversity, improvement, enjoyment/fun, loyalty, credibility, honesty, innovativeness, teamwork, excellence, accountability, sincerity, empowerment, quality, efficiency, dignity, collaboration, stewardship, empathy, accomplishment, courage, wisdom, independence, security, challenge, influence, learning, compassion, friendliness, discipline/order, generosity, persistency, optimism, dependability, flexibility.

Try and identify three values which are the most important ones to you.

Living your values

If you are serious about building up special, trusting relationships with your clients and want to gain the real value of values by living according to your values, then invest a few minutes in the following exercises:

Think about the past week keeping in mind your three top values which you identified above.

- Over the past week have you acted true to your values in how you have **treated others**?
- If so, how?
- If not, how could you have done so? How then would the outcomes have been different in the short-term? And in the long-term?

- Over the past week have you acted true to your values in how you have **made decisions**?
- If so, how?
- If not, how could you have done so? How then would the outcomes have been different in the short-term? And in the long-term?

Now – three challenges!

Today (and every day) make sure you apply at least one of your top three values in the way you treat others

This week (and every week) make sure you apply at least one of your top three values in the way you make decisions

This month (and every month) make sure you apply at least one of your top three values in the way you treat yourself

And finally, a thought to leave you with…I couldn't have put it better myself:

"Values are like fingerprints. Nobody's are the same, but you leave 'em all over everything you do." *Elvis Presley (1935-1977)*

Rose Aghdami, a Chartered Psychologist with over 20 years experience, helps people achieve outstanding results in their personal and professional lives by applying useful psychology in practical and productive ways.

By drawing on her psychological expertise, she encourages clients to develop and nurture high quality, trusting relationships within business, to provide solid, enduring foundations for long-term success.

She helps clients to define and implement their values and strengths, resulting in bringing out the best in themselves and in others so that they become extraordinary leaders of extraordinary teams. This also enables key executives to 'go the extra mile', sustaining high level performance under pressure and over time as business gets tougher than ever.

Rose has been a speaker at several international conferences, she is often recommended by the British Psychological Society as an expert psychologist for media interviews and was the resident psychologist for BBC Radio Oxford for some years.

rose@roseaghdami.com

www.roseaghdami.com

Chapter Twelve
Realistic and Achievable Goals Don't Work
By David Hyner

Realistic and achievable goals do NOT work....
Top achievers set MASSIVE goals!

"Can you name me one thing of man or woman kinds greatest ever achievements that would have been achieved if they would have set realistic and achievable goals?" – Jules Morgan (design engineer, entrepreneur, world powerboat racing champion)

In fact Tim Watts, founder of Pertemps, one of Europe's biggest recruitment companies said;

"I set BIG, fat hairy goals", and when I told him how most people set "realistic and achievable" goals, he laughed and said "you mean we're setting people up for mediocrity... AT BEST !?"

How big ... or MASSIVE are your goals ?

Now before I go off on one about how your goals "should" be massive, may I clearly state that nobody should tell you what your goals should be as one persons MASSIVE is another persons average ... he said resisting the obvious but hilarious innuendo available.

"YOU DECIDE !"

The super successful set massive goals and frequently achieve them, so why do we set mediocre targets?

During my numerous research interviews with top achievers I discovered that massive goals lead to a massive and almost entirely positive change in thought, behavior, and actions taken.

However, before even a metaphorical ball is kicked in the pursuit of their massive goals, highly effective people have a sense of purpose about their goal (I think of it as a "big enough reason WHY" they must obtain their goal) that they have a desire or reason to succeed that outweighs any doubt or fears they may harbor. We have all seen speakers that are very slick yet remain unconvincing to us?

Then we have seen people who represent a charity or foundation and despite their fear of speaking in public and their lack of skills and experience, they hold the audience in the palm of their hand using natural charisma, passion, gesture, body language, tonality and facial expression. They speak with such conviction and heartfelt honesty that you never doubt a word they say.

The difference?

... they had a MASSIVE goal, and a purpose bigger than their fear.

Most people or businesses have great motivation at the start of their goal, but all too soon become weary of the battle and too easily give in, using any excuse as a get out clause, whereas those with a big enough purpose tend to more easily laugh off adversity and steel themselves for challenges, almost knowing that they will end up victorious.

Can you imagine anyone challenging the pharos of ancient Egypt when the very first great pyramid was muted as a goal?

A certain death awaited those who questioned, despite the fact that the rock was to be moved many miles without transport, it was to be a precision engineered build without cranes or large machinery, calculators or surveyors, and that it took thousands of people, many years to build.

One man with a purpose can defeat any army.

What if, you were to find out if your team could break records this year, or you could start making a difference to others right now rather than it be a dream to be actioned awaiting your retirement?

What if you were better than you think you are?

In our keynotes and workshops we give people the skills, systems and confidence to achieve their own massive goals, and many do just that.

"success isn't about being no1. Success is about when it is freezing cold and throwing it down with rain and you chose to go training rather than go to the pub with your mates" – Mark Eccleston (wheelchair sport phenomenon)

I am reminded of one such inspiring woman who I first met in a hotel hallway. She was of petite frame which was bent over as she leant on two walking sticks with supports for the arms. Her face was etched with pain as each and every step seemed to take all of her energy. She made her way down the long hallway towards the training room where I was due to give a keynote talk on setting MASSIVE goals. I walked with her assuring her that the speaker would not start without her being in the room. Her name was Lynn Grocott.

Lynn's life story was one of adversity, abuse and illness. After being sexually and physically abused by her own father, Lynn developed too much of a liking for drink and drugs, before being diagnosed with MS (multiple-sclerosis). MS is what for a few years confined her to the prison of pain within her bedroom. Lynn experienced all this (and other issues that I will not share in this book) and yet on one day, made a decision that she deserved more.

My talk went very well, and in it I shared how successful people set MASSIVE goals and break their goal down into "bite sized" or "realistic and achievable" steps, whereas most people and companies set realistic goals and achieve mediocrity (… at best!)

I finished the talk by suggesting that the delegates decide what they are capable of achieving rather than allow other people to decide for them. I asked them to consider the quote " I DECIDE !"

On the back of this advice, Lynn decided not to allow her condition and situation to hold her back any longer. She got an amazing coach to train her in coaching skills and NLP (neuro-linguistic-programming). Then, Lynn re-learnt how to swim and did a sponsored swim to raise money to build a mother and baby unit in Africa.

She wrote a book about her life story (titled "cut the strings") and began giving talks in schools to young adults.

Within a few short years Lynn had become a qualified coach and master practitioner of NLP. She coached people over coming challenge and adversity and made a genuine difference to the lives of many challenged young people.

Lynn raised enough money to build the mother and baby unit in Africa which to this day bears her name. She published her book which has inspired many other people to change their life and to consider how valid their "reasons/excuses" are.

As a speaker she receives standing ovations most places she speaks and draws tears of both joy and sadness at most events.

She achieved her MASSIVE goals by breaking down the big and scary goal, into daily tasks and smaller goals that she knew could be achieved. She also had a big enough purpose that was far bigger than her fears of failure. Lynn built a support team around her, and used her charm to get expert mentors on areas where she needed help or improvement.

Could you or your company do this?

I think so.

We have all seen football matches where a high flying club have faced a lower league team in a cup match and been given no hope of success by all of the so called "experts".

Yet, despite having a smaller squad of players, fewer fans, less money, less ability, resources and tactical awareness, and against all of the odds, the lower division team win.

Why?
How?

Because they had a MASSIVE goal with a big enough desire/purpose to back it up. For this one game every player pulled the shirt on with more pride than normal. They put differences aside and played as a team, giving 200%, not missing a tackle, and throwing their bodies into situations where normally they might have pulled away.

Their goal was so big (to defeat the bigger club) that nobody gave them a chance so they had no fear of failure.

What assumptions do you make about yourself or your business?

What assumptions do your clients, team, friends or family make about you or your business?

What if they made their assumptions based upon what you "show them to be true"?

What if it were our negative and self doubting actions, attitudes and behaviors that limited their expectations of our performance?

And ... what if we showed them who we really are and what we really can achieve?

I can recall as if it were yesterday when I used our powerful goal setting system for the first time.

Never having set a MASSIVE goal in my life before and never having fundraised for charity either, I decided to see if my system would work by doing a charity event for a local cancer research appeal.

Their previous single biggest event had raised £48'000 profit (awesome eh?).

As a volunteer, with only my spare time, no experience and using an unproven goal setting model they nearly laughed in my face when I suggested that I wanted to raise £50'000 in one event at my first attempt.

I did not raise £50'000!

With the help of a dedicated support team we raised £288'000 !!!!!!

And… in the following six year period, we broke four charities fundraising records raising approximately half a million pounds in the process whilst achieving some of our personal lifetime dreams and ambitions.

What are you or your team, business, family or organization putting off doing because of assumptions and excuses that simply do not stack up under scrutiny?

What is true?
That is all you can ever work with…. The truth !

Why not you?
Why not your business?
Why not now?

What if you could?

"YOU DECIDE !"

key points;
1.Have a purpose bugger than your fears
2.Set MASSIVE goals
3.Break the massive goal down into realistic and achievable steps
4. Find out how real your excuses are

an audio of our goal setting system can be purchased from
www.goalsettingaudio.com

David Hyner is an international professional speaker, researcher, author and broadcaster based in the UK.
Using his 16+ years of research interviews with top achievers as his platform he gives delegates and clients the skills and confidence to set and achieve MASSIVE goals.

Studying the systems, processes, thoughts and behaviors of top achievers makes David a unique speaker as he delivers content of huge value in a fun, challenging and memorable style.

David speaks globally to between 10'000 and 50'000 people a year to audiences ranging from CEO's, conference
audiences and students.

Contact Details:

info@stretchdevelopment.com

www.davidhyner.com

www.stretchdevelopment.com

www.goalsettingaudio.com

Chapter Thirteen
Chase Your Passion, Not Your Pension
By Nigel Risner

"When you are in the room, Be in the room, then we will begin"- Nigel Risner

Evelyn Glennie is renowned as the first lady of solo percussion. She performs 120 concerts each year and has recorded nine albums. Evelyn is profoundly deaf.

She started to lose her hearing at the age of 10 and due to severe nerve damage was profoundly deaf by the time she was 12. Her goal was to become a percussion soloist and in order to perform she learned to "hear" music differently from others. She played in stocking feet and could tell the pitch of a note by the vibrations she felt through her body and her imagination.

She applied to the prestigious Royal Academy of Music in London and despite opposition to her admission by some teachers and was finally admitted and went on to graduate with the academy's highest honours.

Just because her doctor had made a diagnosis that she was profoundly deaf, it did not mean that her passion could not be realized.

One of my favorite tennis players – Andre Agassi – is my hero for reasons other than his prowess on a tennis court. Agassi picked up a tennis racquet at the age of two and his dream was to be the No.1 player in the world and despite on-court tantrums and well documented off-court antics he finally made it.

Like so many before him, after struggling a life time to achieve his goal, when he made it he lost focus and started to drift. In a surprisingly short period of time, his ranking started to slip and eventually took him all the way down to no. 141. He could have given up, but instead he chose to win again. Achieving what you have always dreamed of is often not quite what you expect and unless you visualize and plan for success it can easily slip through your fingers. Agassi lost grip of his dream and lost it all.

More than anything else, it was the loss of his drive to win that ultimately cost him his dream; he didn't know where to go next and so he started fall back. He was lost inside the reality of his own 'dream come true.' To be more exact he had allowed himself to lose sight of 'why' he used to win. He came to his senses and realized that he wanted success again, but he knew that it was going to be a long, painful road back to the top. He had to fight to get back into the habit of winning, of wanting to win. Given how far he had fallen, it was something that very few people would have the courage to do. He was determined.

Dropping down a league, to the Challengers Series, and playing in front of crowds of 1 – 20, against opponents ranked 120 – 1000, he clawed his way back into the game, but this time with renewed purpose and newly ignited passion.

He did not go back to basics, he went forward to basics (Peter Thompson a good friend, taught me that). Within 18 months he was back at No.1, married to Steffi Graff and had enough sponsorship to guarantee his future. He remains a top 10 player today, long after most of his contemporaries have retired and are playing in the Senior's league. He is everything a winner should be; passionate, determined and humble.

What do you do when your sales are slipping, or your kid is constantly misbehaving and getting into trouble at school? Do you start doubting your abilities and avoid the issue (most of us are expert at distracting ourselves from the task in hand) or do you give up? It's not always easy to give up – especially if the problem is your child, but you can give in to doubt and give up in your heart long before you give up the physical effort. The effects can be devastating on you and everyone around you.

If what you are doing is truly your passion could anything stop you from doing it? Just one thing: you.

Without passion, purpose means nothing. Without purpose passion is utterly wasted.

Chase your passion, not your pension

We all know that if we follow our hearts we won't regret what we do, but how many of us actually do anything about it? Is how you spend your days the way you would like to spend them, or is it how you feel you 'have' to live your life? Are you in a self-imposed life sentence of making-ends-meet? If you are living a life without real passion then you have given in to laziness. You're done.

Responsibility is not an excuse for giving up on our dreams, but it is the one we all tout as the root cause of malaise. "I'd love to do that, but how can I when I have got the kids, the mortgage and what about retirement to take care of?" Living today is a very tiring business and the energy it takes – or so it would seem – to make changes is often overwhelming. My god, how would you go about changing your career without jeopardizing your family's security? If your dream is to be a potter and you are the CEO of a large corporation the shift in income would be unbearable. I'm a realist I know what giving up financial security is all about – I lost it all once and I know what it feels like to worry about where your next meal is coming from.

Even when my life was turned upside down I still had something to shoot for. I didn't care that I was driving my Bentley around (yes, I was the original 1980's yuppie) as a taxi cab. I would have cleaned the streets and flipped burgers if that is what it would have taken me to get back on track. I had a plan, I had a purpose, and I was and am completely passionate about what I want from life. Step by step I changed the way I lived. I managed to keep my house, I put my kids through school and together as a family we are all living the lives we want. We did it together. It took compromise and patience, but in the end I have got where I wanted to be at this point in my life.

If throwing pots is what you want to do. Get organized. Get some purpose in your life and start following your passion. You may well be financially secure, you might not: it doesn't matter. You can be just as trapped in your life when you have all the money you need, as you are when you have nothing. The point is, if you are that CEO who longs to toil over a potter's wheel, the pain of not having that in your life is probably crippling you emotionally.

For many sacrificing a dream is a very private misery, as most people are frightened to share their dreams with their family for fear of unbalancing them. Imagine how much better you would feel going to work each day if you knew that working in that job was just one part of your life plan to get you in front of that wheel? Your family will more than likely embrace the fact that you want to do that (if they don't then you need to ask why not?), they help you get there; one step at a time. Earn enough to build your own studio – even if it takes ten years – and maybe while you are doing it go and lease time in an established studio so that you can throw pots while you wait. Spend your time wisely study from masters, learn your craft, build up a portfolio, exhibit your works. Gradually over time you will realize your dream. You will not have compromised the security of your family, but you will have lived your life for you as well as them. When you are old they won't thank you if you tell them you gave up on yourself for them. Nobody would want that on their conscience.

One of my dear friends is tormented by the fact that her mother loves to paint, has always wanted to paint, but just won't do it. Even now, retired and financially secure she won't spend the money she worked so hard to acquire on herself. She is saving it for the inheritance she thinks she needs to leave. I can understand that kind of commitment – anyone with kids can – but when your kids are pleading with you to 'spend it, live your life, leave nothing but good memories behind' what could she be waiting for? After many long months of persuading she has finally started to take art classes and her success is beginning to drive her on. Maybe it wasn't the fear of her children's security that kept her back. Maybe it was the fear that she couldn't do the very thing she loved and that would be too much to bear after all this time of dreaming about it. Chasing your dreams, no matter how small the daily steps you may take to get there are, is a scary, emotionally risky business. Remember why we don't want to step outside our comfort zone? Is what you are currently working on worth giving up on yourself for? Even your kids aren't worth that. Blaming everyone else for your sacrifice is a nonsense that has to stop right now.

Think back through the years and ask yourself who do you remember and why? Apart from your family and friends, the people we tend to remember are normally those individuals who are filled with energy and enthusiasm for life. People who live for themselves make incredible life partners.

If it hurts when you think about the fact that you aren't doing the thing you love or living the life you have always dreamed about, then you owe it yourself and everyone else in your life to change. Do you think you would be a happier person if you were living for your dreams? I would bet my house on the fact that you would be a better person to live with. You may never reach your goal, but the value of your life will increase exponentially when you start living for your dreams.

When people free themselves creatively, everything else miraculously starts to improve. Happiness breeds success. When you chase your passion, your pension will very likely take care of itself. At work people might come to know you as the 'mad potter', but they will respect you for having a go and for doing things differently. You never know you might inspire them to try something for themselves. Creating IMPACT in your life means teaching people how to treat you, which in turns means showing them all the good things about living the way you live.

If you can demonstrate as a CEO that it is OK to have a passion other than your work and that it is possible to manage both successfully, imagine what that would do for the people who work in your company? Just think how much productivity would increase if only an extra 25% of your staff came to work happier because in the evening they lived for themselves and when they came to work, they were 'in the room' and working through that part of their life plan. We can all share in the positive energy of following your passion. Dreams should not be confined to the privacy of your own heart. Like a lost love, or a missed opportunity living without passion can haunt you forever. Don't do that to yourself. Acknowledge your past, park it, then embrace your dreams and let passion flow through your veins. Tomorrow does not have to feel like today. Start living right now. Just say to yourself, 'my name is John, I am CEO, I am a Dad, but really I am a potter.'

Finding purpose in all that passion

Dreaming alone won't get you where you want to be. It takes work, hard work and determination to make your dreams come true – no matter how grand or modest they are. It takes guts to step up and be counted for what you really want in life. Even if your passion in life is your kids and all you want is more respect from them – you have the power to get that. Respect is earned; maybe you haven't been making the right kind of 'deposits' in their emotional piggy banks lately. Would they love you any less if you shared your dreams with them, even asked them to help you? There is nothing wrong in asking for help – even from our kids. They will love you for it. That doesn't mean you can lean on your kids, but asking a person to give your their love and support is empowering for everyone concerned. If you need to make time for your family, then you have to discover how to do it without compromising the other things you like about your life. Life is about compromise, but that should never be the expense of the quality of your own life.

"That's easy for you to say!"

Not really. I still wrestle with the balance between what I want and what I have to do to keep my family alive and well, but I have found my passion and purpose. My family is part of that and I know that getting what I want, means giving them what they want – my purpose is my passion and vice versa. I don't begrudge the time I have to spend doing things I don't really enjoy, because I get to do so many of the things I really want and often it is my family who benefit from the things I would rather not do. I feel content, even in the face of disaster, because I make sure I learn how to move on. The only successful way to embrace your passion is to get a basic 'plan' – have a purpose.

Like all the books on time management tell us, break your task down into bite-size pieces and you will get it done. Spend too long thinking about the enormity of the whole task and you won't get anything done. The same is true of making changes. You can't do it all in one night; anything worth doing is worth toiling for. Yes, we need to visualize success, but we also need to imagine completing the small steps that will get you where you long to be. Finding your purpose doesn't necessarily mean creating a detailed project plan that has to be worked out each week in detail (but it would be another great way to put off change….imagine the hours you could spend working out your life plan!). Finding your purpose is much easier than that. Here is a quick exercise which might help you get there.

Write down the answers to the following in the front of your new success journal.

What is my passion?
What are my bite size goals?
What mechanism will help me get there?
What Action do I need to take?
What will the result look like?
Is this my truth?

When you have the answers to these, you will have your purpose guide. Don't burden yourself with unrealistic time lines. Just know roughly where you need to be and start working towards it. Successful people have many things in common and we can learn a thing or two from looking at what makes them tick.

These are the five things you'll find every successful person has in common:

1.   They have a dream
2.   They have a plan
3.   They have specific knowledge or training

4.   They're willing to work hard

5.   They don't take no for an answer

Remember: Success begins with a state of mind. You must believe you'll be successful in order to become a success.

The following is a list of the skills, talents and characteristics you'll find in people who make an IMPACT.

Successful people have a dream – they have a well-defined purpose. They have a definite goal. They know what they want. They are not easily influenced by the thoughts and opinions of others. They have willpower. They have ideas. Their strong desire brings strong results. They go out and do things that others say can't be done.

Remember: It only takes one sound idea to achieve success.

Remember: People who excel in life are those who produce RESULTS not REASONS.

Anybody can come up with excuses and explanations for why he hasn't made it. Those who want to succeed badly enough don't make excuses.

Successful people have enthusiasm. They want to accomplish something. They have enthusiasm, commitment and pride. They have self-discipline. They are willing to work hard and to go the extra mile. They have a burning desire to succeed. They are willing to do whatever it takes.

Remember: With hard work come results. The joy in life comes with working for and achieving something.

Remember: Some people are so poor they can't pay attention.

Successful people are motivated toward achievement. They take great satisfaction in accomplishing a task.

Successful people are focused. They concentrate on their main goals and objectives. They don't get side-tracked. They don't procrastinate. They work on the projects that are important, and don't allow those projects to sit until the last minute. They're productive, not just busy.

They work on Number 1.

Successful people learn how to get things done. They use their skills, talents, energies and knowledge to the fullest extent possible. They do the things that need to be done, not just the things they like to do. They are willing to work hard and to commit themselves to getting the job done.

Remember: Happiness is found in doing and accomplishing, not in owning and possessing.

Successful people take responsibility for their actions. They don't make excuses. They don't blame others and they don't whine and complain.

Successful people look for solutions to problems. They're opportunity minded. When they see opportunities they take advantage of them.

Successful people make decisions. They think about the issues and relevant facts, give them adequate deliberation and consideration, and make a decision. Decisions aren't put off or delayed, they're made now!

Success Tip: Spend more time thinking and planning before you make your decision, and you'll make better decisions.

Success Tip: When you don't get the expected results from the decision you've made, change your course of action. Decisions should never be carved in stone.

Successful People Have the Courage to Admit They've Made a Mistake. When you make a mistake, admit it, fix it, and move on. Don't waste a lot of time, energy, money, and/or other resources trying to defend a mistake of a bad decision.

Remember: When people are wrong, they may admit it to themselves. If they are handled gently and tactfully, they may admit it to others and even take pride in their frankness and broad-mindedness. But people become very defensive and angry when others try to cram their mistakes down their throats.

Successful people are self-reliant. They have the skills, talent, and training that is needed in order to be successful.

Successful people have specific knowledge, Training and/or Skills and Talents. They know the things they need to know to be successful. And when they need information, knowledge, or skills and talents that they don't possess, they find someone who does possess them.

Successful people work with and co-operate with other people. They have positive, outgoing personalities. They surround themselves with people who offer them help, support and encouragement. They are leaders.

Successful people are enthusiastic. They're excited by what they're doing and that excitement is contagious. They draw people to them because these people want to work with them, do business with them and be with them.

Many years ago I was asked "Nigel, do you like pleasing habits or pleasing results? As I pondered that probing question, and squirmed in my chair like a worm at the end of a hook, I felt as if I had painted myself into a corner. A few moments later I answered: "I like pleasing results". From that moment on my life changed. I began to do the things that were difficult, because they enabled me to achieve my goals.

It's one thing to unearth your dreams and put them on paper, it's quite another to put it into action. Keep your dream in your waking consciousness; learn to enjoy imagining your success and how you will achieve it. Constantly ask yourself 'is what I am doing right now going to get me where I need to be?' If it isn't then you have to ask yourself why you are doing it. That is not the same thing as doing things that might not 'light your fire' if they need to be done to make your dream a reality. If the only means you have to make money to feed your kids and pay the bills is a drag, then the only way to bear the wait until you reach your goal is to keep that goal in mind. You might say to yourself, 'yes this sucks, I hate being a CEO, but tonight I have got a pot to throw in preparation for my first amateur competition, and it keeps my family safe and warm.' When the more tedious things in life are positioned correctly it is amazing how much extra energy you can find for them. Most of the time the only reason we really hate doing something is because there is nothing else going on in our lives worth 'living for'.

Make a promise to yourself that you will create a life you think is worth really 'living' in.

Passion and Purpose – Summary

If you aren't going to be passionate about it, don't do it

Don't deny your dreams.

Chase your passion, not your pension

Find purpose in your passion; let your purpose be your passion. If what you are doing right now is not in alignment with the bigger picture then stop doing it.

Nigel's career began when he was 16 years old when he joined a Commercial Finance Company. After a spell of Tennis Coaching in Israel, he returned to the UK to set up his own Independent Finance Brokerage at the age of 21 with the total sum of £12.80 capital.

With massive growth that made him one of the youngest CEO's he subsequently brought his partner out for £1.5 million and raised equity finance of approximately £2.5 million.

After securing venture capital his Company Milbourne become the largest independent brokerage in the Country.

This became the first of many companies that Nigel set up. He has not only had the experience of working with people but dealing with challenges that thankfully most people have not had to experience. When the financial crash in the late 1980's occurred, instead of complaining he did the one thing that he now teaches all Chief Executives to do – take a risk and do something completely different.

He started mini-cab driving in his Company Bentley until such time as he set up a new business. These events have now given him all the tools to show companies and their staff how to emerge in difficult situations. All his presentations are inter-active, memorable and most importantly life changing.

For further details on how to book Nigel contact nigel@nigelrisner.com

www.nigelrisner.com

Final Thoughts

If you love what you do and do what you love miracles can happen Matsha Sinatar wrote "do what you love and the money will follow It may not happen tomorrow but if you are chasing your passion the rewards will come

Chasing money as we have seen with the majority of lottery winners have not given most of them the happiness they thought

Why am I saying this ,because when I do what is my FIT,AND MY PURPOSE MY LIFE SEEMS TO WORK
When I'm chasing the fee's (whilst its nice)it doesn't give me the same satisfaction.

If you are reading this book ,it means that the 13 people who are co-authoring this book took up the challenge, completed the challenge and defied the odds of the majority of people.
They decided that their passion was to enlighten the world with shared Knowledge. I'm not disputing that when the book becomes the success they are aiming for they might be rewarded ,it wasn't their primary reason for writing this book

So what is this challenge i am talking about?

21 days before this book got published I said to group of speakers that what we could do to inspire, educate a massive amount of people is to collaborate not compete with each other and spread a message of hope, inspiration so that more people achieve their life dreams

What most people do is talk about it as the quote says "when all is said and done much more is said than done"

I'm always concerned whether people are committed to their commitments
Just saying I'm going do it is not the answer
Statistically only seven percent follow through to completion.

Will you be one of the 7 percent?

So now you know how this book was completed
A goal is a dream with a deadline
What do you want to achieve

What's holding you back
Who's holding you back

If it is to be

It is up to me

The ten most powerful two letter words I know.
Nigel Risner.

Printed in Great Britain
by Amazon.co.uk, Ltd.,
Marston Gate.